RAND NATIONAL SECURITY RESEARCH DIVISION

National Intelligence University's Role in Interagency Research

Recommendations from the Intelligence Community

Judith A. Johnston, Natasha Lander, Brian McInnis

Prepared for the Office of the Secretary of Defense

This research was sponsored by the National Intelligence University and conducted within the Intelligence Policy Center of the RAND National Defense Research Institute, a federally funded research and development center sponsored by the Office of the Secretary of Defense, the Joint Staff, the Unified Combatant Commands, the Navy, the Marine Corps, the defense agencies, and the defense Intelligence Community under Contract W74V8H-06-0002.

Library of Congress Cataloging-in-Publication Data

Johnston, Judith A.
  National Intelligence University's role in interagency research : recommendations from the intelligence community / Judith A. Johnston, Natasha Lander, Brian McInnis.
    pages cm
  Includes bibliographical references.
  ISBN 978-0-8330-8051-6 (pbk. : alk. paper)
  1. Intelligence service—United States. 2. National Intelligence University (U.S.)—Research. 3. Interagency coordination—United States. I. Lander, Natasha. II. McInnis, Brian. III. Title.

  JF1525.I6J62 2013
  327.1273--dc23   2013026918

The RAND Corporation is a nonprofit institution that helps improve policy and decisionmaking through research and analysis. RAND's publications do not necessarily reflect the opinions of its research clients and sponsors.

Support RAND—make a tax-deductible charitable contribution at www.rand.org/giving/contribute.html

RAND® is a registered trademark.

© Copyright 2013 RAND Corporation

RAND OFFICES
SANTA MONICA, CA • WASHINGTON, DC
PITTSBURGH, PA • NEW ORLEANS, LA • JACKSON, MS • BOSTON, MA
DOHA, QA • CAMBRIDGE, UK • BRUSSELS, BE

www.rand.org

Preface

The Center for Strategic Intelligence Research (CSIR) of the National Intelligence University (NIU) is responsible for supporting faculty and student research efforts and coordinating NIU research activities with the Intelligence Community (IC). To further its coordination efforts, CSIR was interested in learning more about potential interagency research partners and how collaboration could be improved in ways that would be beneficial to both NIU and the collaborating agency. However, a challenge lies in the fact that research being conducted regularly in the IC exists, for the most part, in small pockets scattered throughout a number of different IC agencies.

CSIR asked RAND to conduct a study that would capture information about these research entities, their responsibilities, and their willingness to support interagency research with NIU, which would help CSIR identify collaborative research opportunities, topics, and processes. To address this request, we identified research entities in the agencies of the IC, including NIU faculty, and conducted semistructured interviews to discuss interagency research and collaboration with NIU. The participants represented a purposive sample and were interviewed between September 2011 and January 2012.

It is important to note that, because this study is based on a purposive sample, in part recommended by the sponsor, the results represent the impressions of senior leaders engaged with research entities in the IC and are not generalizable.

This research was sponsored by NIU and conducted within the Intelligence Policy Center of the RAND National Defense Research Institute, a federally funded research and development center sponsored by the Office of the Secretary of Defense, the Joint Staff, the Unified Combatant Commands, the Navy, the Marine Corps, the defense agencies, and the defense Intelligence Community.

For more information on the RAND Intelligence Policy Center, see http://www.rand.org/nsrd/ndri/centers/intel.html or contact the director (contact information is provided on the web page).

Contents

Figures

Tables

Summary

NIU's Interagency Research Challenge

NIU and CSIR have institutional and IC responsibilities with regard to research. As an accredited institution of higher learning, NIU has an obligation to support faculty and student research. As the national intelligence university, it has an obligation to foster collaborative research to support all the agencies of the IC. Additionally, NIU is the result of an evolution of ideas in the IC and among its leaders about what a national intelligence university should be. This process began with the formation of the Office of the Director of National Intelligence (ODNI) as a requirement of the Intelligence Reform and Terrorism Prevention Act of 2004 (IRTPA).

The official formation of a national intelligence university began in 2006, as noted in IC Directive (ICD) 1.[1] Prior to February 2011, NIU had at least three different leaders, was considered a "virtual" institution, and was chiefly focused on the human capital aspect of intelligence analysis. In addition, from 2006–2011, NIU was besieged by a number of controversial issues and lost a great deal of credibility across the IC. In spite of this, a number of ICDs state the role of NIU in ensuring that IC members are trained on the topics contained in the directives. For example, ICD 501 orders that the NIU, "in collaboration with IC elements, develop community-level information-

---

[1] Intelligence Community Directive 1, *Policy Directive for Intelligence Community Leadership*, May 1, 2006.

sharing training to promote understanding and individual responsibilities with regard to this directive."[2] The current manifestation of the national intelligence university was officially established in February 2011, when the former National Defense Intelligence College (NDIC) was changed to NIU. Interestingly, this change came via Department of Defense Instruction 3305-1. CSIR was originally a component of NDIC and was part of the transfer from NDIC to NIU.

The evolution of NIU resulted in two major institutional challenges: the need to change perceptions within the IC, and the need to establish NIU's role and responsibilities within the IC. Although NIU has a 50-year history of exclusively military intelligence education,[3] it is now committed to educational excellence for the entire IC. Additionally, NIU awards master's degrees every year to students who have completed thesis research. Currently, these students work with CSIR and NIU faculty to determine research topics and locations in the IC where they can conduct their thesis research. There are no formally established collaborative relationships for this purpose.

To help NIU and CSIR address their charge of conducting interagency research, we conducted a survey of entities within the IC that either produce or consume research to gain insight into where collaboration activities might take place, what types of collaboration would be feasible, and what the potential topics for research are. Within the agencies of the IC, there are a number of what we have termed *research entities*—offices, divisions, units, or groups that conduct research. (Appendix B offers a list and descriptions of these entities.) Because research is the primary focus of these entities (although some are responsible for additional mission tasks in analysis, operations, support, etc.) we

---

[2]   Intelligence Community Directive 501, *Discovery and Dissemination or Retrieval of Information Within the Intelligence Community,* January 21, 2009.

[3]   The Defense Intelligence School was established in 1962. It was renamed the Defense Intelligence College in 1983, and civilians were included as students. In 1993, the institution was renamed the Joint Military Intelligence College, devoted solely to intelligence education and research (no training courses). In 2006, the institution's name was changed to the NDIC.

determined that concentrating on these entities would yield meaningful information with regard to interagency research collaboration.

Our Methodology

We determined that data collection should involve interviews with a purposive sample of representatives who lead or manage the IC research entities related to intelligence analysis topics. With CSIR, we identified potential candidate entities and representatives. We conducted the interviews using a semistructured instrument developed with assistance from RAND's Survey Research Group. We used thematic analysis, a qualitative method, to determine themes and patterns in the interview responses. We also consulted the literature on industry-academic partnerships to identify best practices and lessons learned that would inform our results and recommendations.

Findings

Our findings were based on interview feedback from representatives of nine of the 13 possible research entities within the IC, including members of the NIU faculty and leadership. The interview data were analyzed in terms of the four major constructs included in the interview instrument: the research entity's context, the research entity's needs, the research entity's perception of NIU's role, and the research entity's suggestions for NIU regarding collaborative activities. We use these categories as a framework for our discussion of findings and recommendations.

Research Entity Context. We found that the majority of the research entities are small (less than 10 full-time staff); have a number of responsibilities, with longer-term analysis and research being secondary to short-term analytic responses; and have tasks and production requirements that can vary from the identification of emerging trends and threats to knowledge management to planning and hosting conferences intended to build relationships with experts outside the IC. The competing needs of long- and short-term research represent a resource gap that might be addressed by NIU student or faculty researchers.

Research Entity Needs. The research entities, faced with the competing demands of many critical, time-sensitive tasks, small staffs, and limited resources, stated the need for more opportunities to conduct longer-term, strategic research and analysis. Interview participants suggested that NIU should investigate and implement research plans that complement IC goals and requirements (i.e., topics that are before the National Intelligence Managers [NIMs] and the National Intelligence Council (NIC) and are aligned with national priorities). The participants were also interested in having more access to NIU research products that might complement the research being conducted by their entity.

Research Entity Perceptions of NIU's Role. The responses of the participants indicated that they still perceive NIU as a Defense Intelligence Agency (DIA)/military intelligence institution. The participants were cautious about accepting NIU as the IC's educational institution because of NIU's history and evolution (prior to February 2011), and because official guidance has been unclear about NIU's role, particularly regarding authority and the schoolhouses that exist in most of the agencies.

Research Entity Suggestions for NIU Regarding Collaborative Activities. The participants did support the notion of a national intelligence university and were willing to provide limited support for a number of academic activities (e.g., guest lectures, student mentoring, providing potential thesis research topics). However, they also had expectations of what NIU should provide to the IC. They felt that NIU should take the lead in facilitating research collaboration across the IC and between the IC and academia. They were also interested in being able to access more of NIU's research. Finally, the participants stated that NIU should cultivate a more diverse student population, especially in terms of the ability to do strategic analysis, which was seen as a future need of the IC.

Themes Across Responses. In addition to the findings above, we looked at themes across the participants' responses to identify potential root issues. We found a major theme regarding the perceived relationship between NIU and the research entities, particularly regarding collaboration efforts and determining research topics/agendas. The research entities believed that NIU should be responsible for selecting research topics for its students and faculty that are relevant to the IC (particularly the research entities) and that NIU should take the lead in establishing and maintaining collaborative activities with the IC research entities. NIU, on the other hand, has a responsibility to its students and faculty to support their research interests and allow for academic freedom. As such, NIU needs to have control over shaping its research agenda, which is not exactly compatible with determining research topics based on other entities' preferences. This conflict regarding the perceived direction of power and responsibility (i.e., who should identify topics, who should be accountable for collaborative activities) is at the heart of the challenges NIU faces in executing its research role across the IC.

Recommendations

As a new "version" of NIU emerges, opportunities exist to create and execute actions and processes that will align its image to its vision, particularly regarding interagency research collaboration. Our recommendations focus on key actions and processes that should be part of such an effort as based on our interview findings and literature review. We provide these recommendations in the framework of the four major constructs presented above.

Research Entity Context. NIU and CSIR should use a systematic approach to identify potential collaborators based on student/faculty interest and what is known about the research entity's interests and motivation.

Research Entity Needs. NIU should investigate and implement strategic research plans that represent NIU's vision and the research interests of faculty and students. Additionally, the research plan should complement IC interests, particularly those topics that are before the NIMs and the NIC and are aligned with national priorities.

Research Entity Perceptions of NIU's role. NIU should increase and maintain awareness of community-wide access to NIU research resources.

NIU should formalize its enterprise-wide outreach programs and familiarize each agency with NIU's mission, needs, and resources.

We also recommend strengthening communication and collaboration efforts outside of student research that will aide in clarifying NIU's identity and begin to change perceptions of NIU within the IC to the benefit of all.

Research Entity Suggestions for NIU Regarding Collaborative Activities. Create opportunities for representatives of the schoolhouses and research entities to regularly come together to discuss IC education and training needs and facility collaboration, and consider exploring ways to reduce redundancy in currently overlapping areas.

Themes Across Responses. In our analysis of the interview data regarding NIU and collaborative research, we saw that the IC participants believed NIU should continue to have a passive role in the development of a research program. Participants stated that NIU students and faculty should select research topics based on what is important to the IC, including the research entities.

We recommend that NIU and CSIR adopt an active role in setting NIU's research agenda that is driven by faculty research interests and that may complement priorities and strategic topics of interest at the national level. Adopting an active role—directing the research agenda—will help NIU meet its institutional goals while also allowing it to target and plan relationship development and collaboration activities.

We also recommend that NIU and CSIR develop a framework and methods for formalizing relationships with IC entities that outline the specific roles and responsibilities of the parties involved. Formalizing relationships (e.g., through a memorandum of agreement or memorandum of understanding) will ensure that NIU's and CSIR's requirements are met, as well as manage the expectations of those involved.

Acknowledgments

Conducting the research for this study required candid responses and observations from both the sponsor and the participants. We are grateful to Dr. David Ellison, Dr. Susan Studds, and Dr. Cathryn Thurston for their interest in getting at the real thoughts and impressions of interagency research with NIU, as well as their candor in discussions and guidance throughout the project.

Given the time and resource constraints of the senior leaders and managers of the research entities in the IC, we appreciate the time and thoughtfulness they gave during the interview process.

Our thanks go to Melissa Bradley, who possesses the unique ability to design interview instruments with questions that get at the heart of the issues of interest, and to Kathi Webb, whose creativity of thought, process guidance, and impeccable review capabilities made this report much better. We would also like to thank Carol "Rollie" Flynn and Harry Thie for their insights as reviewers.

Abbreviations

AOI	Analytic Outreach Initiative
CCO	Center for Complex Operations
CIA	Central Intelligence Agency
COCOM	Combatant Command
CSIR	Center for Strategic Intelligence Research
CSNR	Center for the Study of National Reconnaissance
CSR	Center for Strategic Research
DIA	Defense Intelligence Agency
DoD	Department of Defense
IC	Intelligence Community
ICD	Intelligence Community Directive
IFA	Institute for Analysis
INR	Bureau of Intelligence and Research
IRTPA	Intelligence Reform and Terrorism Prevention Act
JWICS	Joint Worldwide Intelligence Communication System
NCTC	National Counterterrorism Center
NDIC	National Defense Intelligence College
NIC	National Intelligence Council
NIM	National Intelligence Manager
NIO	National Intelligence Officer
NIU	National Intelligence University
NRO	National Reconnaissance Office
NTAC	National Threat Assessment Center

ODNI	Office of the Director of National Intelligence
OTR	Office of Outreach (in Department of State INR)
SFG	Strategic Futures Group

CHAPTER ONE

Introduction

In 2005, the Office of the Director of National Intelligence (ODNI) was formed in response to recommendations of the 9/11 Commission Report,[1] four Executive Orders,[2] and the Intelligence Reform and Terrorism Prevention Act (IRTPA)[3] to "forge an Intelligence Community that delivers the most insightful intelligence possible."[4] One of the goals of the ODNI is to promote a diverse, highly skilled intelligence workforce that reflects the strength of the United States. To help address this goal, the National Intelligence University (NIU) was formed.

Since its inception, the NIU has evolved as an institution of higher learning serving the Intelligence Community (IC) by preparing intelligence professionals, through education and research, to serve most effectively in positions throughout the IC, including intelligence

---

[1] National Commission on Terrorist Attacks Upon the United States (the 9-11 Commission), The 9/11 Commission Report: Final Report of the National Commission on Terrorist Attacks Upon the United States, Washington, D.C.: U.S. Government Printing Office, 2004.

[2] Executive Order 13355: Strengthened Management of the Intelligence Community, 69 FR 53593, August 27, 2004; Executive Order 13356: Strengthening the Sharing of Terrorism Information to Protect Americans, 69 FR 53599, August 27, 2004; Executive Order 13383: Amending Executive Orders 12139 and 12949 in Light of Establishment of the Office of Director of National Intelligence, 70 FR 41933, July 15, 2005; Executive Order 13388: Further Strengthening the Sharing of Terrorism Information to Protect Americans, 70 FR 62023, October 25, 2005.

[3] Public Law 108-458, Intelligence Reform and Terrorism Prevention Act of 2004 (IRTPA), 118 Stat. 3638, Sections 1041–1043, December 17, 2004.

[4] Office of the Director of National Intelligence, "Mission, Vision & Goals," undated.

entities in the Department of Defense (DoD). In October 2011, the former National Defense Intelligence College (NDIC) became NIU. This change has allowed NIU to adopt the accreditation, degree seeking, and research programs associated with NDIC since the 1960s. In addition, this change has challenged NIU to extend its standards and reputation for academic research to support all agencies of the IC.

Background

The first iteration of NIU was established in 2005. It was a virtual institution and mostly focused on human capital issues; providing intelligence professional education and development programs for the IC; and building cooperative relationships with schools, centers, and civilian institutions. NIU had at least four chancellors during the short time between 2005 and 2011. During this period, NIU did not demonstrate much progress against its goals, experienced some controversial events, and left the general populace of the IC with a low opinion of its effectiveness.

In 2011, the NIU was transformed by absorbing NDIC, an accredited, degree-granting institution with a 50-year history of providing military intelligence education. NDIC began as the Defense Intelligence School in 1962, was renamed the Defense Intelligence College in 1983, when accreditation was granted, then was renamed the Joint Military Intelligence College in 1993 and the National Defense Intelligence College in 2006. In February of 2011, NDIC was designated the National Intelligence University, with the goal of addressing the need for an accredited educational institution that serves all agencies of the IC in support of the strategic goals of ODNI. As the mission aperture for NIU has expanded, the role of the Center for Strategic Intelligence Research (CSIR), a component of NIU, has also expanded to include addressing the research needs of intelligence professionals in the IC, as well as Combatant Command (COCOM) intelligence professionals, including NIU students and faculty. CSIR, originally a component of NDIC, became part of NIU during the 2011 transformation.

NIU's educational infrastructure makes it well suited to adapting existing capabilities to the needs of the IC, specifically in terms of conducting research on topics that support interagency interests collectively or individually. The corpus of research developed by the research components of DoD provides resources that can be leveraged in support of new topics of value to IC components. As CSIR expands its focus from military intelligence to IC-wide issues, it needs to expand its knowledge of current IC research entities, their missions and objectives, and their resources, so as to identify potential research roles for NIU and CSIR students and faculty. Additionally, CSIR needs to develop a broader network of relationships and a wider range of processes for determining relevant research topics and collaborating within the IC to conduct and evaluate this research.

Study Purpose

For this study, we first captured information about research entities in the IC, their missions, their willingness to support interagency research with NIU, and their representatives' suggestions for research topics of particular interest. We then analyzed this information to assist CSIR in identifying potential collaborative research opportunities and partners, research topics, and processes and activities to facilitate interagency research.

Method

To elicit IC member views on research collaboration with NIU, we conducted semistructured interviews with representatives of the various established think tanks and research units across the IC, which we have termed *research entities*. The criterion for inclusion in this category was simply that the office, division, unit, or group focus on conducting research within the agencies of the IC.

In preparation for conducting the interviews, we created a data collection plan, an interview instrument (provided in Appendix A), and, in collaboration with NIU and CSIR leadership, selected a sample of research entities and identified senior representatives to be interviewed. We also determined major interview constructs that would allow us to identify the mission, objectives, products, resources, and perceptions of the interviewees.

We examined primary sources and other extant data to inform our recommendations for supporting the conduct of interagency research, including collaboration strategies and processes for implementing an interagency research agenda.

Organization of the Report

Chapter Two presents information about the research entities derived from our interviews with senior representatives of various IC research entities. It also includes findings from the research literature, along with best practices, predominantly from business literature, that are relevant to successful research partnerships. Chapter Three presents the results of our study and the patterns, threads, and commonalities we identified in our analysis of these results. Chapter Four presents recommendations for NIU and CSIR consideration and proposes methods and processes for implementing these recommendations. Finally, Chapter Five presents our concluding observations, particularly regarding the challenges NIU and CSIR will face in establishing its research role in the IC.

CHAPTER TWO

Data Collected: Interviews and Literature

Interview Participants and Their Research Entities

The IC consists of seventeen separate components: ODNI, the Central Intelligence Agency (CIA), the Defense Intelligence Agency (DIA), the National Geospatial Intelligence Agency, the National Reconnaissance Office, the Department of State, the Department of the Treasury, the Federal Bureau of Investigation, the National Security Agency, Air Force Intelligence, Army Intelligence, Coast Guard Intelligence, the Department of Energy, the Department of Homeland Security, the Drug Enforcement Agency, Marine Corps Intelligence, and Navy Intelligence. Working with NIU and CSIR, we identified 13 research entities in nine of these 17 components.

This study was designed to elicit expert opinions from those familiar with IC research entities that focus on intelligence analysis–related research. We were able to speak with senior leaders representing nine of the research entities identified. Our study participants were senior IC leaders of entities responsible for research production and/or consumption. The distribution of these participants across agencies is shown in Figure 2.1.

To complement our interviews and get a clearer picture of the types of research entities that exist in the IC, their missions, and the environments in which they work, we gathered data from online sources and built brief descriptions of these research entities. All the research

Figure 2.1
Distribution of Study Participants, by Agency

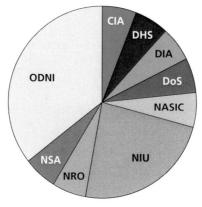

NOTE: DHA = Department of Homeland Security; DoS = Department of State; NASIC = National Air and Space Intelligence Center; NRO = National Reconnaissance Office; NSA = National Security Agency.
RAND *RR243-2.1*

entities we identified within the IC are described in Appendix B. Those research entities that participated in our study are listed in Table 2.1.

Based on the descriptions we developed of the IC research entities, we identified four broad, mission-focused categories to serve as a framework for understanding these entities and for contextualizing our interview data. The variety in the structure and mission focus (i.e., the research interests) of these entities highlights the complexity of NIU/CSIR's mission to identify and promote interagency research.

The mission-focused categories we identified are: (1) conduct strategic analysis, (2) advance analytic tradecraft, (3) outreach, and (4) social science and historical research/lessons learned. In some instances, the research entity fit into more than one category. We offer brief descriptions and examples of each of these categories below to serve as background for considering our interview data.

Conduct strategic analyses. The research entities with this mission strive to address mid- to long-term research objectives on topics mainly of importance to the National Intelligence Managers (NIMs) and national priorities. Research entities with this mission include the National Intelligence Council (NIC) Strategic Futures Group (SFG),

Table 2.1
Participant Research Entities and Their Agencies

Research Entity	IC Component
Center for the Study of Intelligence	Central Intelligence Agency
Office of Intelligence Analysis	Department of Homeland Security
Director for Analysis, Research Director	Defense Intelligence Agency
Bureau of Intelligence & Research, Office of Research	Department of State
CSIR, NIU leadership, NIU Faculty	National Intelligence University
Center for the Study of National Reconnaissance	National Reconnaissance Office
Institute for Analysis	National Security Agency
National Intelligence Managers	Office of the Director of National Intelligence
NIC Strategic Futures Group	Office of the Director of National Intelligence
Office of Analytic Outreach	Office of the Director of National Intelligence
National Counter Terrorism Center	Office of the Director of National Intelligence

the NIMs, the Office of Intelligence Analysis of the Department of Homeland Security, the Center for Strategic Research (CSR) at the Institute for National Strategic Studies of the National Defense University, and the Center for Complex Operations (CCO).

Develop new tradecraft and innovative methods for intelligence problem solving. Research entities with this mission are focused on how intelligence analysis is conducted (i.e., tradecraft) and how to improve the substance, quality, and reliability of this analysis. Such research entities include the Directorate for Analysis (DI) Research Office (including the Devil's Advocate and Analytic Ombudsman programs) at DIA and the Institute for Analysis (IFA) at NSA.

Promote and conduct analytic outreach. Research entities that focus on analytic outreach are concerned with identifying and leveraging outside expertise to contribute to, critique, or otherwise improve intelligence analysis and products. Analytic outreach is the focus of entities such as the Office of Outreach at the Department of State Bureau of Intelligence and Research (INR) and the Analytic Outreach Initiative (AOI) at ODNI.

Social science and historical research/lessons learned. The Center for the Study of Intelligence (CSI) at the Central Intelligence Agency and the Center for the Study of National Reconnaissance (CSNR) at the NRO have unique roles in the IC that involve social science and historical research on individuals, organizations, operations, and programs. They also conduct scholarly studies that focus on lessons learned from strategic, operational, and tactical perspectives; studies of emerging trends; and knowledge-sharing conferences and seminars. CSNR focuses on topics that are relevant primarily to NRO. CSI is responsible for lessons-learned studies for CIA, as well as ODNI, making the variety of research topic areas quite broad. The CCO (DoD, Department of State, U.S. Agency for International Development) focuses on research, lessons learned, and ways to enhance training and education for planning and executing interagency operations. Groups that study lessons learned also exist in most of the agencies of the IC.

Common Operating Environments

Among the research entities studied, we found several common defining factors. The majority of research entities (78 percent) had ten or less full-time staff but had varied responsibilities, as described above. In addition, these entities are responsible for creating a number of different products that can vary by topic and scope. Finally, the operational tempo of these entities is brisk, leaving little time for strategic analysis of their own efforts—a perceived need. Given the responsibilities of these entities, their resources, and their constraints, it would seem that they are likely targets for the development of interagency research activities with NIU.

Interview Agenda

Our interviews were aimed at addressing four major constructs, along with a number of subtopics for each.

Research Entity Context. We asked interviewees to describe their offices' missions and objectives. We also discussed what resources (i.e., personnel, financial, information, or technology) might be needed to better serve their customers and carry out their missions. We then asked the respondents about the type of products (i.e., briefings, summaries, in-depth studies) their offices provide to customers and whether these products can be shared easily within the IC, outside the IC, or both.

Research Entity Needs. We asked participants to explain how their research agendas are constructed. In particular, we were interested in learning if research topics are predetermined and, if so, what they are based on (e.g., customer request or specific national priorities). In light of how research topics are determined in a particular research entity, we asked participants to tell us about the topics on their wish lists (i.e., the research topics that are of great interest to the research activity and/or the IC in general but cannot realistically be addressed due to resource constraints), as well as topics that have an audience within the IC, but are typically benched when higher priority products are requested from customers.

Research Entity Perceptions of NIU's role. We asked participants how they were familiar with NIU—through colleagues, as a student or faculty member/guest lecturer, through interactions with faculty and/or programs, or other prior experience. We elicited further details regarding their perceptions of NIU's role in the IC based on their experience, including any strengths or weaknesses they observed during the course of their involvement with NIU.

Research Entity Suggestions for NIU Regarding Collaborative Activities. As part of every interview, we asked participants to provide recommendations to NIU for fulfilling its mission. These recommendations focused both on support to NIU from the research activity and support from NIU.

Chapter Three will present the findings from these interviews.

Lessons from the Literature

To provide additional support to our research findings and identify additional related considerations that may provide insight to our recommendations, we consulted business and academic journals, related professional society reports, and websites. We focused on best practices and lessons learned from other types of partnerships that resemble interagency partnerships, such as partnerships between academic institutions and private industry or government entities.

Given that NIU is trying to introduce a new image along with new interagency activities, we also looked at research regarding changing perceptions. The topics below emerged as areas for further investigation from our interviews, discussions with the study sponsor, and the initial key findings from our data.

Forming Partnerships with Collaborators—Turning Lessons Into Practice

The literature about forming and maintaining research partnerships between entities with one or more shared interests provided some helpful insights for our study. Our review of this literature was limited to identifying the important elements of successful industry-academic partnerships. Most examples of such relationships are between pharmaceutical companies and academia, biotechnical companies and academia, and information technology companies and academia.[1] In these relationships, both entities benefit. Industry acquires the specialized scientific skill set—often not resident in the firm—of experts and students without having to commit to hiring full-time staff. Academia

---

[1]   B. A. Lameman, M. S. El-Nasr, A. Drachen, W. Foster, D. Moura, and B. Aghabeigi, "User Studies—A Strategy Towards a Successful Industry-Academic Relationship," conference paper, Futureplay, 2010; New York Academy of Sciences, "Academic-Industry Collaboration Best Practices," conference proceedings, December 8, 2009; C. Reiger, "Models for Academic/Industry Partnerships," presentation made at the Center for Research on Information Technology and Organizations, University of California, Irvine, February 13, 2008; Business–Higher Education Forum, "Working Together, Creating Knowledge: The University-Industry Research Collaborative Initiative," Research Collaboration Initiative Task Force, undated.

has the benefit of funded research opportunities for faculty and students. Opportunities for student employment sometimes result as well.

We chose the industry-academic partnership as a framework because of the similarities between an industry-academic partnership and the IC-NIU relationship. In a sense, the IC writ large can be seen as sharing many characteristics with business in the partnership and NIU can be seen as sharing characteristics with academia. Like the IC, industrial environments have a broad range of operational considerations, with research being just one. Further, they are responsible for the integration of new research into the firm and the customer base. It is likely that their research interests are broader than those pursued within an academic partnership. Like NIU, the academic partner is focused on conducting quality, meaningful research that aligns with its research agenda, as well as providing learning experiences for its students and faculty. The academic partner also has commitments to academic freedom that may conflict with industry interests.

Best practices indicate that the identification of collaborative partners should be conducted systematically, keeping in mind specific goals and objectives. The following criteria are recommended when considering candidate collaborative partners. In the case of an IC-NIU partnership, the following are criteria that both the IC and NIU should consider:

- Will the experience that results from the collaborative effort enhance the student's education and support the institution's vision of the future?
- Will this experience add to the student's knowledge of the use of research methods, as well as the subject matter?
- Will this experience provide opportunities for the student to increase his or her professional network?
- Will this experience further academia's ability to provide high-performing researchers whose abilities match and/or strengthen the partner's needs?

Once an industry-academia partnership is formed, best practices suggest that the following critical issues and questions should be addressed as early in the process as possible:

- Determine what drives the partnership. Will the combined capabilities of the partnership fill a gap, or is it necessary to address a particular research question or domain?
- Determine how the partnership will account for cultural differences. For example, how can an IC-NIU partnership reconcile the IC's drive to accomplish mission objectives and NIU's commitment to academic freedom while respecting both?
- Assuming the synergy between research and education is important because it supports job readiness, does the partnership bridge the theory and practice gap?
- How will the partnership measure success?

These best practice recommendations—based on the experiences of industry-academic research partnerships—underscore the importance of forethought, careful planning, and organizing discussion during the development of research partnerships. Accepting the similarities between industry-academic partnerships and IC-NIU partnerships, it becomes apparent how these best practices could be applied.

Changing Perceptions and Attitudes—What Leads to Success?

A challenging issue as NIU attempts to establish its role within the IC is that of changing the IC members' perceptions of NIU. As stated earlier, the identity of the NIU in the IC has been unstable and its reputation is of a less-than-successful institution. Therefore, it is understandable that members of the IC have an unclear view of NIU, its role in the IC enterprise, and its role as a driver of interagency research. Unfortunately, these perceptions can be difficult to change.

Research shows that the formation of perception relies on feedback between what people perceive and what they expect, and that people's expectations and beliefs further create a predisposition to see things in a certain way.[2] Perceptions shaped by drive or motivation and/or expectations can result in people interpreting ambiguous data so that it appears unambiguous.[3] In the case of NIU, examples of ambiguous data would include changes in the description of NIU, such as changes regarding its relationship with the IC schoolhouses; the separation of an Assistant Director of National Intelligence position from the Chancellor of NIU; adopting a different physical concept of NIU (e.g., a virtual versus a brick-and-mortar campus); or replacing one institution with another (e.g., replacing NDIC with NIU). Members of the IC will likely retain the impressions they formed about NIU based on their first exposure to it. And when changes are made that do not seem to fit with their original impressions, they will ignore the ambiguous data or interpret it so that it does fit.

Attitudes are formed by experiences and perceptions of experiences.[4] Changing or overcoming perceptions and impressions, even those based on ambiguous data, can require a number of external conditions—behavior modeling of a respected figure, expectancy of success associated with desired change, opportunities to demonstrate the changed perception or attitude, and opportunities for feedback on successful performance.[5] Perception change, depending on how it is formed and how permanent the change is anticipated to be, can require a much greater effort than the persuasion techniques common to marketing activities.

Clearly, implementing measures to successfully, positively affect perceptions requires a significant commitment that should figure prominently in the decisionmaking process. Resource restrictions may not allow for a robust effort. However, smaller-scale activities may have

[2]   F. H. Allport, *Theories of Perception and the Concept of Structure*, New York: Wiley, 1955.

[3]   J. S. Bruner and L. Postman, "On the Perception of Incongruity: A Paradigm," *Journal of Personality*, Vol. 18, 1949, pp. 203–223.

[4]   Allport, 1955.

[5]   A. Bandura, *Principles of Behavior Modification*, New York: Holt, Rinehart and Winston, 1969; R. M. Gagne, *The Conditions of Learning*, New York: Holt, Rinehart and Winston, 1985; R. M. Gagne and M. P. Driscoll, *Essentials of Learning for Instruction*, Englewood Cliffs, N.J.: Prentice-Hall, 1988.

an impact with the persistent support of NIU faculty and students. An awareness of NIU's history and current roles and responsibilities, as well as a sensitivity to its roots and the reputation it has in the IC as a defense intelligence institution can guide the NIU faculty and students in their interactions within the IC as ambassadors of NIU and stewards of the NIU message.

Findings

We conducted interviews with 18 senior leaders representing the IC research entities and NIU either in person or by telephone. We conducted interpretational/thematic analysis on the interview data, yielding findings that we categorized into four major constructs (matching the constructs of the interview instrument) and 13 sub-constructs. We then looked at themes across the interview responses to identify root causes and/or issues. Our findings will be discussed first in terms of the constructs and sub-constructs identified in Table 3.1, and then by the themes we identified across responses.

Table 3.1
Constructs and Sub-Constructs for Data Categorization

Construct	Sub-Constructs
Describing the context of the research entity	Mission Objectives Resources Products
Understanding the research entity's needs	Product wish list Unaddressed research topics
Perceptions of NIU's role	Perceptions Prior experience Strengths Weaknesses
Collecting participant suggestions for NIU regarding collaborative activities	Support from NIU Support to NIU Other activities

Describing the Research Entity Context—Findings

The research entities represented in this study were generally small in size (78 percent had ten or fewer full-time staff members) but varied in terms of their mission, objectives, and products. The research entities fell into one or both of two mission categories: traditional intelligence analysis and knowledge management. Where the mission was traditional intelligence analysis, objectives included identifying emerging technology, trends, and risks and advancing analytic tradecraft. The objectives that fell under the knowledge management category were information sharing within the IC and outreach between the private sector, academia, and the IC.

The products developed by the research entities varied greatly:

- To meet the objective of identifying patterns and risks of emerging trends, products included recommending and/or conducting relevant studies—both near-term and strategic—as well as making contributions to longer-range, high-visibility studies such as the National Intelligence Estimates.
- Products geared toward advancing analytic tradecraft or improving information sharing in the IC included support to professional development activities, the identification of tools and analysis methods, conducting gap analyses, and examining past and current practices via lessons learned studies.
- The products for facilitating outreach between the IC and outside experts included relationship building; conducting conferences; generating papers and reports (including conference proceedings); identifying new data, data sources, and subject-matter experts; and sponsoring academic research projects.

In summary, the IC research entities can be characterized by having a small staff, a mission that involves various objectives met through the production of a number of different products. In addition, the operational tempo of these entities is brisk, leaving little time for strategic analysis of their own efforts.

Understanding Research Entity Needs—Findings

The research entities, particularly those reported as having ten or fewer full-time staff, were faced with the challenge of having insufficient time and manpower to address their competing needs: near-term, critical, and/or tactical analysis versus longer-term, strategic research and analysis. Interview participants expressed the need to more regularly address emerging concerns and trends in intelligence analysis. The ability to increase staff was limited and access to additional research support (via NIU thesis students or research fellows) would fill what seemed to be a nagging and consistent void. Current research relationships between NIU/CSIR and the IC are generally of an ad hoc nature. Student and/or faculty research topics are driven by individual interest, and they partner with whoever is willing.

Participants expressed a desire to have a greater awareness of and convenient, timely access to NIU research activities and products. Knowledge of NIU research was seen as helpful for identifying work that might complement or inform their research efforts.

Perceptions of NIU's Role—Findings

Among the participants in this study, the perception still persists that the "new" NIU is solely a DIA/military institution. Many members of the IC see military intelligence analysis as very different from intelligence analysis in the nonmilitary elements of the IC. They are concerned that this difference in perspective and, to a degree, culture, will hinder NIU from becoming fully relevant to needs across the IC. Additionally, the history of NIU in ODNI prior to February 2011 made some of the study participants doubtful about the effectiveness of or need for a national intelligence university. Many participants were unsure of NIU's educational role versus the training/professional development roles of other agency-based "schoolhouses."

Finally, participants stated that the physical location of NIU, which was perceived as far away from many of the IC agencies, was a deterrent to in-person collaboration.

Participant Suggestions for NIU Regarding Collaborative Activities—Findings

All participants offered suggestions regarding NIU's role in the IC and NIU's pursuit of interagency research efforts. These suggestions were directional—some of them had to do with the research entities providing support to NIU, while others focused on NIU providing support to the research entities or the IC writ large.

Support to NIU. The participants were willing to support NIU in academic activities. Many of the participants were willing to sponsor student research, provide thesis topics, and provide mentoring. One participant was willing to teach a course and three were willing to conduct guest lectures. The break out of the types of support offered and frequency of offers made by study participants is shown in Figure 3.1. The frequency shown in the figure represents all offers of help. Some participants offered more than one type of support.

Part of our interview tool centered on research topics that might be relevant for NIU students. About 40 percent of participants reported

Figure 3.1
Type and Frequency of Support Suggested

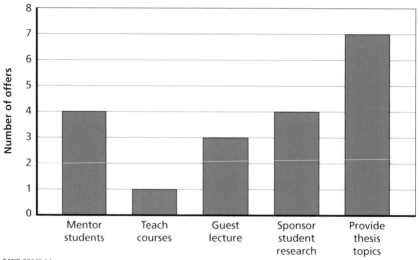

that, if asked, they would be willing to provide potential research topics. While the participants identified no specific topics, the majority of participants recommended that the research be derived from topics under study by NIMs and the NIC and be aligned with identified national priorities.

Participants suggested and were willing to support other NIU-related activities that were focused on increasing interagency collaboration. These suggestions included helping to identify audiences and fora for student presentations, as well as supporting access for NIU students and faculty to IC fora. Other suggestions ranged from the very broad (e.g., supporting NIU outreach activities) to the somewhat narrow (e.g., posting links to NIU websites on the research entity's classified research websites, including summaries of student theses in IC publications).

Support from NIU. Participants also had expectations about support from NIU. In the interviews, participants also provided a number of broad expectations from NIU that would the benefit the IC. Among these expectations, participants proposed several roles/responsibilities for NIU in the community. These suggestions focused on interagency collaboration (facilitating collaboration across the IC), helping to make the analyst population more diverse, acting as a bridge between the IC and academia, and sharing research products.

Themes Across Responses

As we analyzed the data across responses, one significant theme emerged. In discussions of NIU's role in interagency research, there was a distinct, directional perception of the relationship between NIU and the IC research entities underlying most remarks. The perception is focused on responsibility and, perhaps, power. The participants saw NIU as the driver for most of the efforts discussed, with the expectation that NIU is mindful of research entity and IC needs. For example, the research entity representatives believed that NIU should be responsible for selecting research topics for NIU students but wanted the topics to be relevant to the research entities' unspecified needs. The research entities supported the idea of collaborative research but felt that the bulk of the collaborative effort (identifying partners, determining topics, setting up necessary agreements) should rest with NIU. The research entities were willing to support NIU activities but did not express a willingness to take the lead on any of them. The way forward for NIU will include decisions regarding this perceived relationship and ways to ensure success.

CHAPTER FOUR

Recommendations

Our study participants were positive in their discussion of NIU and they provided a number of suggestions that addressed CSIR and NIU more generally. The suggestions focused on how NIU and CSIR could help address the needs and resources of their own research entities, and on what NIU should do. The recommendations that follow are based on the findings of our interviews with senior leaders in the IC.

Our recommendations are presented in terms of the four constructs that frame this study. The interviewees recommended a wide range of activities that would, indeed, support the research entities but may not meet NIU's needs. Rather than suggest a laundry list of activities that would meet needs in a somewhat one-sided way, we recommend actions that should help build a strong foundation for the new instantiation of NIU. The challenges to building an interagency research capability are discussed in Chapter Five.

Describing the Context of the Research Entity— Recommendations

NIU/CSIR Should Use a Systematic Approach to Identifying Potential Research Collaborators

By constructing and implementing a systematic approach, NIU could use its knowledge of the research entities' context—their missions, interests, and constraints—to identify IC candidates for collaborative research or research support activities. Such a systematic approach would include

- an examination of research topics to find a confluence between NIU-relevant topics, NIM/NIC-relevant topics, and research entity–relevant topics
- analysis to determine the appropriate product scope (e.g., a long- or short-range topic, an existing or emergent topic)
- establishing the role of the NIU researcher and the type of activity that would best benefit both NIU and the research entity.

NIU/CSIR Should Use a Stepwise Development Model for Creating Partnerships

Upon identification of a potential collaboration activity and collaboration candidates, NIU would reach out to representatives of the identified entities, either through a formal presentation or informal meetings, to discuss potential research projects that would be useful for both parties. As part of these discussions, NIU should reflect on the following best practice questions relating to partnership:

- What drives the partnership?
- How will the partnership account for cultural differences?
- Does the partnership bridge the theory and practice gap?
- How will the partnership measure success?

Agreements to pursue interagency research or other collaboration efforts should be formalized, possibly through a memorandum of understanding or memorandum of agreement.

To establish its own best practices for developing partnerships, we recommend that NIU create a stepwise model, focusing first on the development of a particular partnership model for research (e.g., partnership between IC and NIU/CSIR) and then using a successful iteration of that model to inform the development of other partnerships (e.g., with industry, other academic institutions). In the development of the first model, special attention should be paid to lessons learned, as well as to processes for formalizing relationships and responsibilities with new partners.

Additional efforts to foster interagency research partnerships could include

- making faculty, students, and prospective students aware of interagency research partners and topics under study
- conducting regular group meetings with IC partnership representatives at rotating locations to identify additional research topics of common interest and potential new partners.

Understanding the Research Entity Needs—Recommendations

NIU Should Investigate and Implement Research Plans That Complement IC Goals and Requirements and Are Aligned with National Priorities

The current nature of research topic selection for NIU/IC collaborations is generally ad hoc, and is managed by whoever is willing to support it. It is possible to use such a model to identify research topics for interagency collaboration with NIU. However, ad hoc topic selection based on the identification of pockets of IC support may serve to deconstruct NIU/CSIR's research agenda. Also, this process can limit the type of research conducted, the topics addressed, the number of relationships and opportunities created for students, and the stability and growth of NIU/CSIR's research portfolio.

While considering the research requirements of other IC entities will help collaboration efforts, NIU student and faculty research should take priority. To best serve the research community, we recommend that NIU develop an overarching strategic research agenda that takes into consideration faculty and student research interests, national priorities, and major issues that have the attention of NIMs and the NIC. Creating such an overarching research framework would support and simplify research topic selection for NIU and would help ensure that the research is relevant to one or more of the IC research entities.

Research Entity's Perception of NIU's Role— Recommendations

NIU Should Formalize Its Enterprise-Wide Outreach Programs and Familiarize Each Agency with NIU's Mission, Needs, and Resources

By formalizing NIU's outreach program and educating the IC, NIU has the opportunity to get its message out. How regularly and frequently NIU reaches out to the community should be considered in terms of the educational impact it wants to have.

Participants showed a preference for having web-based access to information about NIU via the Joint Worldwide Intelligence Communication System (JWICS). Therefore, it is important that NIU ensure it has a significant online presence with up-to-date resources and information and uses platforms that maximize access for IC agencies. Maintaining a research blog, a newsletter, or an information portal focused on areas of potential involvement with NIU and including a mechanism for interested parties to respond could help open doors for interagency involvement. The success of such an approach would, of course, depend on the IC members' awareness of its existence.

Student and faculty participation in IC blogs and/or analyst exchange sites could subtly expose NIU to a wider audience while also increasing networking opportunities for the NIU participants.

NIU Should Increase and Maintain Awareness of Community-Wide Access to NIU Research Resources

The participants of this study were very interested in having access to a wider variety of NIU research products. The motivation was that NIU research products might complement the research entities' work, providing a building block for additional research. While NIU/CSIR has an active plan in place to make past and current theses available, the perception exists that not much of NIU's research is available across the IC. Currently, only certain research products are available to the rest of the community, and the paths to access these products are not well known. In addition to creating greater awareness of the availability of student and faculty research, NIU should consider how and where to provide access to additional research products. At the same time, specific criteria should be developed to determine the selection and suitability of student research for publication. The criteria for publication could reflect the objectives for student education and research at NIU, and selection results could provide valuable feedback information on this topic.

If a research entity's specific interests are known to NIU—perhaps through systematic analysis, as discussed earlier—NIU should consider ways to connect that research entity with relevant NIU research directly.

Providing the IC access to a greater number of student and faculty research products presents an additional resource burden. NIU might tap members of the IC to support the review of potential research for relevancy to IC interests, as defined earlier, and to provide input regarding the selection of products for broader circulation from an IC perspective.

NIU Should Focus on Strengthening Communication and Collaboration Efforts Outside of Student Research

Communication and collaboration activities will aid in clarifying NIU's identify and help with perception issues in the IC regarding NIU's roles.

NIU should consider providing frequent reminders of NIU activities through a network that is commonly used by the IC (e.g., A-Space, or an NIU information portal) to reach across the IC, engage a number of interested persons, and ensure that the NIU stays on the radar in an environment where there is competition for time and resources.

Participant Suggestions for NIU Regarding Collaborative Activities—Recommendations

Given NIU's responsibility as a collaborative agent, the emphasis in the IC on developing collaborative efforts, and the enterprise-wide reality of insufficient time and resources, it is not surprising that the participants in this study looked to NIU to take on the lead role in developing IC collaborations.

NIU should engage IC representatives, particularly those representing IC research entities, in NIU programs regularly. Creating an awareness of milestones in the academic calendar, opportunities and/or needs for guest lecturers or subject-matter experts, and the support of faculty/fellow/student research can open up opportunities for engaging others in the IC. Another possible form of engagement would be to conduct a series of topical seminars that are particularly relevant to current national priorities and NIC and NIM areas of analysis. Rotating the host location of in-person events or employing videoconferencing technology would foster a sense of equity and collaboration, as would requests for post-event feedback.

NIU Should Create Opportunities for Representatives of Schoolhouses and Research Entities to Regularly Discuss IC Education and Training Needs, Facilitate Collaboration

Nearly every agency in the IC has its own schoolhouse for agency-specific training and preparation. While NIU's original responsibilities included oversight of these schoolhouses, the current instantiation of NIU does not maintain this responsibility. However, there is a certain sensitivity among some of the schoolhouses stemming from confusion or apprehension about who might have decisionmaking power over them. It would be useful for NIU to create opportunities for and facilitate regular discussions among representatives of schoolhouses and research entities regarding training needs, collaborative opportunities, and possible ways of reducing the redundancy in education and training areas that currently overlap. This activity could include the establishment of enterprise-wide standards for IC intelligence education programs. In this role, NIU can help shape IC training and education without threatening agency autonomy and help prepare for the day when funding shortages lead to the centralization or reduction of IC education and training.

NIU Should Consider Building Its Role as an Academic Hub for Practitioners of All Levels

Identifying and incubating special topics or skills in tradecraft or other intelligence functions could help develop NIU's role as an academic hub for practitioners. NIU could also act as coordinator for working groups or other groups authorized to operationalize skill or topic development, offering student and faculty support, as well as a physical meeting space.

CHAPTER FIVE

Concluding Observations

As a dual-hatted organization in the IC with both institutional and community obligations, NIU faces a number of challenges when embarking on interagency research and other collaborative activities. One benefit to this position is that NIU, unlike many of the entities it will be partnering with, has visibility across the agencies of the IC and a broader view of IC needs and research interests. This visibility can inform research decisions that serve NIU's current and future educational goals and vision for intelligence analysis education and support IC research needs holistically.

This chapter addresses the challenges to expanding NIU engagement in interagency research.

Challenge: Enterprise-Wide Understanding of NIU's Role

First and foremost among these challenges is ensuring, to the greatest extent possible, that members of the IC have a clear understanding of NIU and its charter.[1] Our study results revealed a lingering impression that NIU, because of its roots as a military intelligence college, is focused solely on military intelligence education and has limited relevance to the IC enterprise. This is compounded by the fact that DIA, a military intelligence agency, currently houses and is the executive

---

[1] Under Secretary of Defense for Intelligence, Department of Defense Instruction 3305.01, December 22, 2006, Incorporating Change 1, February 9, 2011.

agent for NIU, with oversight from the Under Secretary of Defense for Intelligence.

In February 2011, NDIC which was colocated with DIA on Joint Base Anacostia Bolling, was designated the NIU. As stated earlier, there were at least three prior incarnations of NIU, which focused mostly on human capital issues and suffered from a number of controversial problems. The current incarnation comes with a 50-year history of exclusively military intelligence education.

The previous incarnations of NIU, beginning in 2005 and stemming from the recommendations of IRTPA,[2] called for an NIU system that would draw together the existing IC schools and training centers and provide centralized management and common educational standards through a virtual model rather than a brick-and-mortar institution. At that time, the Chancellor of NIU was also the Assistant Deputy Director of National Intelligence for Education and Training. Several subsequent Intelligence Community Directives (ICDs) defined very specific responsibilities of the chancellor that were heavily focused on human capital issues.[3] In addition, other ICDs (e.g., ICD 501[4]) began to include directives that charged the chancellor of NIU with developing shared, community-level training to promote an understanding of the individual responsibilities related in these directives. However, NIU's agency over the IC schoolhouses was not sustained as a responsibility.[5]

Depending on exactly when, since 2005, an individual or agency interacted with or learned about NIU, they will have a different perception of NIU that may or may not have changed since. To facilitate collaboration, NIU needs to address this challenge. There are a number of options that could be used to address this, each with varying scope. There is no compelling evidence to show that a large campaign would have more success or impact than a smaller effort. However, NIU

---

[2]   Public Law 108-458.

[3]   Intelligence Community Directive 610, *Competency Directories for the Intelligence Community Workforce,* September 1, 2008.

[4]   Intelligence Community Directive 501.

[5]   Under Secretary of Defense for Intelligence, 2011.

should remain cognizant of the challenges tied to misperceptions about its role and take every opportunity to educate their colleagues in the IC.

Challenge: Collaborating in a Disparate Research Environment

A second challenge is determining effective methods for collaborating with research entities that would support NIU's research interests and identifying which research entities in the IC would benefit from NIU's assistance. Currently, the research entities reside within their own agencies and there is little organizational "glue" connecting them. To move interagency research forward, relationships must be built to help identify commonalities among research entities and the benefits to collaboration/collaborators. Awareness of this common ground will help increase communication and awareness, serving to strengthen the bond.

The organizational glue could take one of a number of different forms from the informal (e.g., an IC Community of Interest for Interagency Intelligence Research) to the formal (securing ODNI leadership support for identifying research entities in the IC as Centers of Intelligence Research Excellence). The precise form the organization would take depends on what outcomes are desired and what level of support for the idea exists among IC leadership and the community itself. It is possible that a government Working Group could be established to determine how an IC Interagency Research Group would be structured, what its responsibilities would be, and how its success would be measured.

Challenge: Finding a Balance When Setting the Research Agenda

Our study participants were positive in their discussion of NIU and they provided a number of suggestions addressed to NIU/CSIR and to

NIU more generally. The suggestions focused on how NIU/CSIR could help address the needs and resources of the individual IC research entities, and on what NIU *should* do writ large. These suggestions propose a passive model in which the NIU/CSIR research agenda is driven by the needs and directives of others in the IC.

NIU's role as an academic institution suggests, however, that it needs to adopt an active model in which the research requirements and interests of NIU faculty and students drive NIU's research agenda and related research activities in the IC (interagency and intra-agency). While NIU research cannot be totally independent from the IC and must consider IC enterprise research requirements, an active model would allow NIU to control the development of its own research agenda rather than being directed by what others think is best.

Setting a research agenda involves a series of decisions, including what topics will be addressed, what research methods and designs will be used, and how research will be conducted and evaluated. These decisions may be made passively or actively. *Active decisionmaking* involves the consideration of two or more alternatives, their possible consequences, and how those consequences are valued and/or prioritized by the decisionmaker. *Passive decisionmaking* also involves a choice, but the decisionmaker allows someone else, time, or chance to make the decision. The models for research agenda setting presented here—active and passive—are so named because of the type of decisionmaking that most closely resembles the method used to set the research agenda.[6]

Figure 5.1 depicts the influences on CSIR in a passive model of agenda setting[7] regarding interagency research. If, for example, the research entities or other elements of the IC determine the topics for collaborative research with NIU based on their own needs and require-

---

[6]   H. A. Simon, "Rational Choice and the Structure of the Environment," *Psychological Review*, Vol. 63, No. 2, 1965, pp. 129–138; P. Slovic, S. Lichtenstein, and B. Fischoff, "Decision-making," in R. C. Atkinson, R. J. Hernstein, G. Lindzey, and R. D. Luce, eds., *Steven's Handbook of Experimental Psychology, Volume 2: Learning and Cognition*, 2nd ed., New York: John Wiley and Sons, 1988, pp. 673–738.

[7]   Figure 5.1 was created with the concept-mapping software *Inspiration 9.0.* This representation is not intended to be exhaustive.

ments, the net result is an NIU research identity that consists of a combination of topics and issues determined by NIU's collaborative partners. In this model, a number of different competing interests can influence or determine the research agenda with little influence from NIU/CSIR itself.

This lack of identity and, in some ways, lack of control, limits NIU's ability to tie the research experiences it offers to students with NIU's vision of student achievement. There is no way to predict accurately which topics the IC entities will request research on, making a reliable agenda challenging. The passive model also makes it difficult to streamline efforts for setting the research agenda because the agenda is always subject to change based on the needs of the IC and individual relationships within the community that are often personality-driven.

Figure 5.1
Influences on Passive Research Agenda Setting

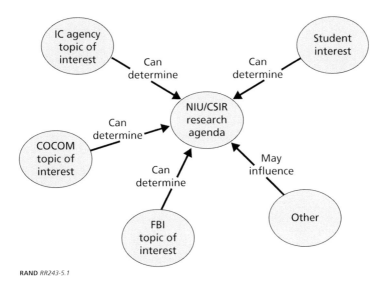

RAND *RR243-5.1*

The active model of research agenda setting, as shown in Figure 5.2[8] for NIU/CSIR, presents a different power dynamic among the influences and drivers. In the active model, NIU/CSIR determines the research agenda. As in active decisionmaking, this model of agenda setting allows NIU/CSIR to consider alternatives and prioritize their consequences to meet NIU's educational goals and objectives. Faculty research and strategic research topics (as determined by NIMs, national intelligence officers (NIOs), and national priorities set by ODNI) are the primary influences on the research agenda and NIU

Figure 5.2
Influences on Active Research Agenda Setting

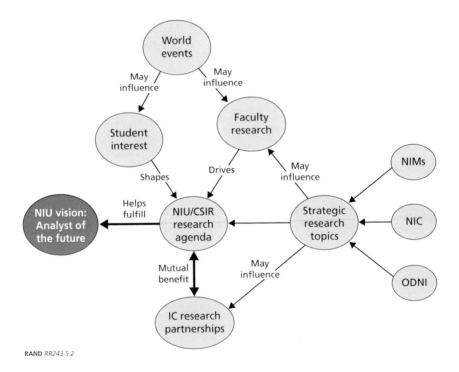

RAND *RR243-5.2*

---

8   Figure 5.2 was created with the concept-mapping software *Inspiration 9.0*. This representation is not intended to be exhaustive.

faculty research programs are the primary drivers. Because NIU/CSIR determines the research agenda, the research topics and requirements can be reliable and consistent. As such, the research agenda that results from this model can help shape student interest and can be crafted to directly support NIU's educational goals and vision for future analysts.

In the active model, IC research partnerships are formed to serve mutual interests and both parties benefit. Maintaining a greater level of control over the selection of collaborative research topics and partners does not detract from the collaboration itself, but enriches it. The adoption of this model requires the engagement of NIU faculty not only to maintain a level of research quality that is consistent with higher education and IC standards but also to ensure that the research agenda stays relevant to both educational and IC purposes.

A comparison of the active and passive models of research agenda setting indicates that the type of model employed, particularly with regard to interagency collaboration, can and will affect more than just who identifies the research topic. It determines who actually controls the process and, in some ways, the outcomes.

Because of its unique role in the IC, NIU will need to strike a balance between these two models to guide the development of interagency research partnerships, the selection of research topics, and other collaborative activities. It can either continue in a passive role and identify ways to temper its shortcomings, or it can adopt an active model with some flexibility, staying mindful of the need to remain relevant to the work of the IC.

Good research builds the reputation and identity of an institution of higher learning. Students, faculty, research partners (IC, academic, industry), and research funders are drawn to institutions that exhibit a strong, easily identifiable research program. At the base of these assertions is the development and maintenance of a research agenda that is actively determined and represents high-quality products. This is the model that most universities and colleges have used to build their research capabilities, their student body, and their reputations. It is one that NIU should consider as it attempts to reach its new goals and objectives.

Interview Instrument

CSIR Interagency Research Study Interview Instrument

1. Research Conducted
    a. How would you characterize research in your unit?
        ○ Is there a specific research agenda for your unit?
        ○ Are research objectives formalized?
        ○ What types of objectives are included (e.g., long-term and/or short-term research goals/plans)?
    b. Who designs and conducts the studies? Who provides guidance?
        ○ Do you have students/interns/etc. engaged in research at your agency?
    c. What/who drives topic selection? What is the process for topic identification/selection?
    d. Are research topics: Internally oriented or customer/externally oriented? Both? Strategic or tactical? Both? Of local interest only? Agency interest? IC interest?
    e. What is done currently with results? Are they published or disseminated in some way?
    f. In your opinion, what are some examples of successful research projects? What made them successful?
    g. What constraints impact your ability to conduct research (e.g., funding, access to materials)?

    h. If you could expand resources to support research in your unit, what resources would you identify?

    i. In the absence of resource constraints, what would your vision be for research in your unit? In your agency? In the IC?

2. Current Initiative—NIU Collaboration/Interagency Research

    a. What do you see as the benefits of this new initiative? For the IC? Your agency? Others?

    b. What information should be conveyed to the IC about this new initiative? To your agency?

    c. What recommendations/ideas can you share about the how NIU faculty and student researchers can best coordinate research efforts or collaborate with the IC? With your agency?

       ◦ What resources are needed to make this successful?

       ◦ How would you like to see this program administered or managed? Particularly the management of the students?

    d. Would this initiative be of interest to your unit/agency? Why or why not?

       ◦ What do you need from NIU to in order to support this initiative (e.g., information on areas of interest, administrative/process/coordination issues)?

       ◦ What topics would be of interest to your agency? In your opinion, what are some examples of research projects that you think would be appropriate topics for NIU students and beneficial to your agency? What makes them so?

       ◦ What resources, if any, could your agency provide to support this initiative? Providing topics? Providing guidance to students? Mentors?

Research Entities in the Intelligence Community

This appendix includes descriptions of a number of research entities in the IC. It is important to note that the predominant definition of research in these centers is, in fact, analysis that focuses on either emerging or strategic topics that are generally outside the scope of the work of discipline-specific intelligence analysts. Research is a systematic, *repeatable* investigation that includes a research question or hypothesis, research design that identifies and employs particular discipline-specific methods for data collection and analysis, results of data collection and analysis, and the impact of the data analysis on the research question or hypothesis. With very few exceptions, the research being conducted by these entities is technically analysis, rather than research.

Analytic Outreach Initiative

Office of the Director of National Intelligence

AOI's purpose is to identify existing outreach activities in the IC, expand their capabilities, and encourage new approaches or best practices to improve their efforts. Membership of the group incorporates representatives from all IC agencies. To meet its goals for outreach, AOI focuses on building collegial ties between members of the IC, as well as promoting different ways for members to engage with each other through outreach activities. Through these measures, AOI intends to promote relationships and professional networks throughout the IC that will advance the community's ability to share knowledge, tradecraft, and craft collaborative analysis. The outreach exercises include conferences, seminars, workshops, scenario exercises, studies, and exchanges all sponsored or lead by AOI. Further, through networking and building "communities of interest," AOI aims to help the IC more readily access shared, unclassified knowledge to solve critical problems. AOI coordinates and supports outreach efforts conducted through the Department of State INR, the executive agent for outreach in the IC.

Center for Complex Operations

Department of Defense, Department of State, U.S. Agency for International Development

CCO is "a Congressionally mandated center located at the National Defense University tasked to conduct research, identify lessons learned, enhance training and education, and improve the planning and execution of interagency operations."[1] It is also responsible for knowledge and information management for training and education related to complex operations. CCO is responsible for enabling networking and coordination among government entities involved in complex operations, as well as the development and maintenance of a complex operations training and education Community of Practice. CCO publishes *Prism* (a journal of security studies relevant to complex operations), the *CCO Case Studies Series* (classroom teaching case studies that focus on complex operations), and a number of books on complex operation subjects. CCO offers a number of unpaid internship positions throughout the year to support its research activities.

Website: http://cco.dodlive.mil/

---

[1]   National Defense University, Center for Complex Operations, home page, undated.

Center for Strategic Research

Institute for National Strategic Studies at the National Defense University

CSR provides objective, rigorous, and timely analysis that responds to the needs of decisionmakers and various policy audiences. The research focuses on emerging strategic trends that pose longer-term challenges for U.S. national security and raise important questions for policymakers. The center focuses on seven core regions and areas of interest: East Asia and the Pacific, Europe and Eurasia, Near East and South Asia, the Western Hemisphere, Africa, Energy and Environmental Security, and Future Strategic Concepts. The center also addresses special projects, including those related to "power and vulnerability in an era of contested dominance."[2] CSR is responsible for a number of publications, including analytic papers, event reports, and analysis and reviews.

Website: http://www.ndu.edu/inss/index.cfm?type=section&secid=52 &pageid=4

Center for the Study of Intelligence

Central Intelligence Agency

CSI is responsible for research, outreach to intelligence practitioners and scholars, and the collection of intelligence material for historical purposes. CSI does not necessarily cover the current intelligence issues that analysts follow but is interested, rather, in how intelligence shapes policy.

CSI has five specific responsibilities to the intelligence community, which are as follows:

---

[2] National Defense University Institute for National Studies, Center for Strategic Research, home page, 2010.

1. Intelligence Research: CSI publishes *Studies in Intelligence*, a journal that is published quarterly in a classified format and annually in an unclassified format. It also publishes books, monographs, and other research on intelligence issues.
2. Intelligence History: CSI publishes written and oral reports on the history of intelligence and the CIA. It also publishes documentaries from the Cold War and supports the State Department's *Foreign Relations of the United States* series.
3. Historical Records: CSI publishes historical records to promote the general public's understanding of intelligence.
4. Conferences and Seminars: CSI sponsors events to make its research widely available. It also creates opportunities to bring practitioners and scholars together and commemorate landmark events in intelligence.

CSI is also home to the CIA and ODNI Lessons Learned programs. Through these programs, CSI produces studies about internal "issues, programs, operations, business practices, and events that illustrate lessons worthy of being preserved and shared."[3] Publications produced by way of these lessons learned programs include, *(U) Relocation of CIA's Iraq Support Base in 2009: Keys to Success*; *(U) Lessons Learned: The National Security Council Staff Rotation—Walking in a Policymaker's Shoes*; and *(U) CIA's Management of Nonofficial Cover Personnel and Operations*.

Website: https://www.cia.gov/library/center-for-the-study-of-intelligence/index.html

---

[3]   Central Intelligence Agency, Center for the Study of Intelligence, home page, March 7, 2013.

Center for the Study of National Reconnaissance

National Reconnaissance Office

CSNR's mission is to promote the study, dialogue, and understanding of the discipline and practice of national reconnaissance. The primary purpose of research at CSNR is to provide an analytical framework and historical context for effective policy and programmatic decisions by NRO leadership. The research focus is on social science and the humanities (history). CSNR's products include organizational and program histories, research articles, symposia, and lessons learned studies. It also publishes scholarly articles, studies, commentaries, and book reviews in *National Reconnaissance: Journal of the Discipline and Practice.*

Websites: http://intellipedia.intelink.ic.gov/wiki/
Center_for_the_Study_of_National_Reconnaissance

http://www.nro.gov/history/csnr/index.html

Directorate for Analysis Research Director

Defense Intelligence Agency

The DI at DIA is positioned to develop analytic methods and trade craft. The Research Director staff is responsible for identifying what gets at research—the tools, methods, and professional activities that support the research mission of DIA and the socialization of analysts within the IC.

The DI is designed to maintain DIA's strategic research efforts. The office also "develops, implements, and evaluates activities and transformation efforts improving analytic quality, tradecraft, and professional development for all of DI's open source analysts."[4] The Research Director's office also houses DIA's Devil's Advocate and Ana-

---

[4]   Defense Intelligence Agency, "DI Research Director," April 2010.

lytic Ombudsman programs, both of which seek to emphasize analytic rigor and the development of well-rounded intelligence analysts.

Website: http://www.dia.mil/about/

INR Office of Outreach

Department of State/Bureau of Intelligence and Research

As the executive agent for outreach in the IC, INR Office of Outreach (OTR) is positioned to "organize and fund conferences and studies to facilitate the interchange of expertise and ideas between outside experts and government officials, leading to a more informed foreign policy process."[5] OTR's external research staff sponsors 200–250 seminars each year that bring together IC personnel and external experts to enhance their collective understanding of foreign policy issues. OTR publishes the results of these conferences as conference papers distributed to the State Department and other U.S. government agencies. They also sponsor research studies that pertain to a specific event or decision. Additionally, OTR houses the Title VIII program on Eastern Europe and the Independent States of the Former Soviet Union, which seeks to develop and maintain U.S. experts on these regions by providing grants for language training, graduate-level studies, and postdoctoral research to interested and qualified recipients.[6]

Website: http://www.state.gov/s/inr/

---

[5]   United States Department of State, INR Office of External Research Staff, "Office Description and Mission," August 12, 2011.

[6]   United States Department of State, 2011.

Office of Intelligence Analysis

Department of Homeland Security

The Office of Intelligence Analysis's capability is primarily focused on intelligence analysis, based on its mission to "equip the Homeland Security Enterprise with the intelligence and information it needs to keep the homeland safe, secure, and resilient."[7] It does this through analysis, collection, information-sharing, and information management. Its analysis activities fall under three categories:

- immediate and ongoing threats
- strategic contexts (context, trends, pattern analysis)
- opportunities (emerging issues for which reporting streams are new or fragmentary).

Based on information provided through its website, about 10 percent of I&A's focus is on identifying new topics and issues that could impact the Department of Homeland Security and its customers.

Websites: http://intellipedia.interlink.ic.gov/wiki/ DHS_Office_of_Intelligence_and_Analysis

http://www.dhs.gov/about-office-intelligence-and-analysis

National Counterterrorism Center

Office of the Director of National Intelligence

The National Counterterrorism Center (NCTC) is designed to support the collection and dissemination of intelligence analysis on counterterrorism measures. Although not a traditional center for research within the IC, NCTC identifies, analyzes, and shares information on counterterrorism so that the leaders in operations and analysis at other U.S.

---

[7]   Department of Homeland Security, "About the Office of Intelligence Analysis," undated.

government agencies can respond to threats more effectively. NCTC research includes the gap analysis of IC-wide counterterrorism needs for research and analysis. NCTC has far-reaching access to U.S. government resources to support counterterrorism planning activities.

NCTC serves as the primary U.S. government agency for analyzing and integrating all intelligence pertaining to terrorism and counterterrorism, with the exception of purely domestic terrorism. In this capacity, NCTC serves as the central, shared knowledge bank on terrorists (known and suspected) and international terrorist groups and is responsible for outreach of this material to agencies and ensuring access to all-source intelligence needed to execute counterterrorism measures.

Website: http://www.nctc.gov/

National Intelligence Council Strategic Futures Group

Office of the Director of National Intelligence

The NIC SFG collects research on global issues and generates analysis on the future strategic environment and emerging risks and opportunities. The NIC SFG is a production environment focusing on strategic research without the geographic or functional area constraints of other agencies. However, unlike the analysis at other agencies, the NIC SFG is a consumer of analysis that it then uses to produce authoritative strategic research on far-reaching issues and trends. One product of this work is the SFG intelligence estimates of emerging technology and threats.

To meet its objectives, the NIC works with senior intelligence consumers to identify their current and future needs and promote collaboration between analysts at each agency in the IC. More broadly, the NIC is the center for mid- and long-term strategic thinking in the IC, and the SFG is a key nexus in meeting that mission.

Website: http://www.dni.gov/nic/NIC_home.html

National Intelligence Managers

Office of the Director of National Intelligence

The NIMs, through ODNI, "oversee and integrate all aspects of the IC's collection and analytic efforts against a particular region or function."[8] The NIMs are organized into 17 regional and functional areas, as shown in Table B.1.

NIMs are designated representatives of the Director of National Intelligence for each area. They are responsible for the design and successful implementation of the Unifying Intelligence Strategies for each region or function.

Website: http://www.intelink.ic.gov/sites/ddii/nim/default.aspx

Table B.1
NIM Regional and Functional Areas

Regional	Functional
Africa	Counterintelligence
East Asia	Counterproliferation
Eurasia	Counterterrorism
Europe	Cyber
Iran	Economic Issues
Near East	Military Issues
Koreas	Science and Technology
South Asia	Threat Finance
Western Hemisphere	

---

[8]   Office of the Director of National Intelligence, "Home – National Intelligence Managers (NIMs)," undated.

National Security Agency

Institute for Analysis

NSA is responsible for producing new processes, methodologies, and techniques for the analytic community. They create these new methods for problem solving by reaching out to industry and academic experts and leveraging previously untapped human capital. IFA works through "challenges" with "challenge champions," who are generally NSA employees who commit to working with the IFA to solve a difficult intelligence problem that is relevant to their office and to the IC. While challenges vary in scope, they generally receive six to nine months of effort.

National Threat Assessment Center

United States Secret Service, Department of Justice

The National Threat Assessment Center (NTAC) mission is "to identify, assess, and manage persons who have the interest and ability to mount attacks against Secret Service protectees."[9] Although NTAC is not traditionally recognized as a center for research within the IC, the organization provides collection, aggregation, and training roles that advance the capabilities of both intelligence operations and analysis. Specifically, NTAC conducts research on potential threats and targeted violence and provides training on their methods to law enforcement and public safety officials. They also engage in information sharing with these partners and promote standardization among all levels of government to investigate threats.

Examples of NTAC's products include *Campus Attacks: Targeted Violence Affecting Institutions of Higher Education*, which was written in response to the April 2007 Virginia Tech shooting; *Safe School Initiative*, a study of school-based attacks at K–12 schools; and *The Insider Threat Study*, a series of reports on illicit cyber activity within the gov-

---

[9]   United States Secret Service, "National Threat Assessment Center," 2010.

ernment, information technology, telecommunications, banking and finance, and critical infrastructure sectors.[10]

Website: http://www.secretservice.gov/ntac.shtml

---

[10]   United States Secret Service, 2010.

References

Allport, F. H., *Theories of Perception and the Concept of Structure*, New York: Wiley, 1955.

Bandura, A., *Principles of Behavior Modification*, New York: Holt, Rinehart and Winston, 1969.

Bruner, J. S., and L. Postman, "On the Perception of Incongruity: A Paradigm," *Journal of Personality*, Vol. 18, 1949, pp. 203–223.

Business–Higher Education Forum, "Working Together, Creating Knowledge: The University-Industry Research Collaborative Initiative," Research Collaboration Initiative Task Force, undated. As of March 18, 2013: http://www.bhef.com/solutions/documents/working-together.pdf

Central Intelligence Agency, Center for the Study of Intelligence, home page, March 7, 2013. As of April 3, 2013: https://www.cia.gov/library/center-for-the-study-of-intelligence/index.html

Defense Intelligence Agency, "DI Research Director," April 2010. As of March 13, 2012: http://intellipedia.intelink.ic.gov/wiki/Research-Director

Department of Homeland Security, "Office of Intelligence and Analysis," undated. As of March 13, 2012: http://intellipedia.interlink.ic.gov/wiki/ DHS_Office_of_Intelligence_and_Analysis

Executive Order 13355: Strengthened Management of the Intelligence Community, 69 FR 53593, August 27, 2004.

Executive Order 13356: Strengthening the Sharing of Terrorism Information to Protect Americans, 69 FR 53599, August 27, 2004.

Executive Order 13383: Amending Executive Orders 12139 and 12949 in Light of Establishment of the Office of Director of National Intelligence, 70 FR 41933, July 15, 2005.

Executive Order 13388: Further Strengthening the Sharing of Terrorism Information to Protect Americans, 70 FR 62023, October 25, 2005.

Gagne, R. M., *The Conditions of Learning*, New York: Holt, Rinehart and Winston, 1985.

Gagne, R. M., and M. P. Driscoll, *Essentials of Learning for Instruction*, Englewood Cliffs, N.J.: Prentice-Hall, 1988.

Intelligence Community Directive 1, *Policy Directive for Intelligence Community Leadership*, May 1, 2006.

Intelligence Community Directive 610, *Competency Directories for the Intelligence Community Workforce*, September 1, 2008.

Intelligence Community Directive 501, *Discovery and Dissemination or Retrieval of Information Within the Intelligence Community*, January 21, 2009.

Lameman, B. A., M. S. El-Nasr, A. Drachen, W. Foster, D. Moura, and B. Aghabeigi, "User Studies—A Strategy Towards a Successful Industry-Academic Relationship," conference paper, Futureplay, 2010. As of March 18, 2013: http://nuweb.neu.edu/magy/conference/BardelSFU_final.pdf

National Commission on Terrorist Attacks Upon the United States (the 9-11 Commission), The 9/11 Commission Report: Final Report of the National Commission on Terrorist Attacks Upon the United States, Washington, D.C.: US Government Printing Office, 2004.

National Defense University, Center for Complex Operations, home page, undated. As of April 3, 2013: http://cco.dodlive.mil/

National Defense University Institute for National Studies, Center for Strategic Research, home page, 2010. As of April 3, 2013: http://www.ndu.edu/inss/index.cfm?type=section&secid=52&pageid=4

New York Academy of Sciences, "Academic-Industry Collaboration Best Practices," conference proceedings, December 8, 2009. As of March 18, 2013: http://www.nyas.org/publications/ebriefings/Detail. aspx?cid=a937b74a-a986-4bff-9633-9afd6d046e85

Office of the Director of National Intelligence, "Mission, Vision & Goals," undated. As of January 20, 2012: http://www.dni.gov/mission.htm

Office of the Director of National Intelligence, "Home – National Intelligence Managers (NIMs)," undated. As of March 13, 2012: http://www.intelink.ic.gov/sites/ddii/nim/default.aspx

Public Law 108-458, Intelligence Reform and Terrorism Prevention Act of 2004 (IRTPA), 118 Stat. 3638, Sections 1041–1043, December 17, 2004.

Reiger, C., "Models for Academic/Industry Partnerships," presentation made at the Center for Research on Information Technology and Organizations, University of California, Irvine, February 13, 2008. As of March 18, 2013:
http://www.crito.uci.edu/critohours/2008/rieger.pdf

Simon, H. A., "Rational Choice and the Structure of the Environment," *Psychological Review*, Vol. 63, No. 2, 1965, pp. 129–138.

Slovic, P., S. Lichtenstein, and B. Fischoff, "Decision-making," in R. C. Atkinson, R. J. Hernstein, G. Lindzey, and R. D. Luce, eds., *Steven's Handbook of Experimental Psychology, Volume 2: Learning and Cognition*, 2nd ed., New York: John Wiley and Sons, 1988, pp. 673–738.

Under Secretary of Defense for Intelligence, Department of Defense Instruction 3305.01, December 22, 2006, Incorporating Change 1, February 9, 2011.

United States Department of State, INR Office of External Research Staff, "Office Description and Mission," August 12, 2011. As of March 13, 2012:
http://intellipedia.intelink.ic.gov/wiki/INR_Office_of_External_Research_Staff

United States Secret Service, "National Threat Assessment Center," 2010. As of March 13, 2012:
http://www.secretservice.gov/ntac.shtml

termeasure once attackers become aware of how they work. For example, malware can detect being located in a sandbox, and wait to execute until on a viable target system; other payloads have a timer enabled that lasts longer than the defender's observation.

Defenders have also attempted to improve the security of their information and systems by changing the very nature of the computing and communication architecture in which they operate. In one approach, defenders physically isolate familiar software and computing instances from open system networks so that they are not accessible to attackers. These are commonly referred to as "air-gap" methods, and they separate the physical networks from the open Internet, making it more challenging to gain entry. This approach is commonly used in networks intended for national security applications, and selectively used in commerce for sensitive applications, such as telephonic switching control. It is relatively expensive because it requires dedicated physical infrastructure, but also relatively effective in keeping out unauthorized users.

A different architectural approach is to change the types of software or computing instances that are used. One such technique is called "moving target defense," in which open-system Internet resources are still used routinely by the defender, but software or server instances are replaced frequently, making it more difficult for attackers to establish malware that will persist long enough to exploit underlying vulnerabilities in the defender systems. While air-gapping and moving target defense are still uncommon, they are representative of hybrid approaches that defenders can use to resist attackers without giving up all the benefits and efficiencies of using Internet technologies for the foundation of their organization information systems.

Figure 3.1 provides a limited overview of some measures and corresponding countermeasures created and used by defenders and attackers.

Figure 3.1
Diagram Depicting the Measure-Countermeasure Dance Between Defender and Attacker

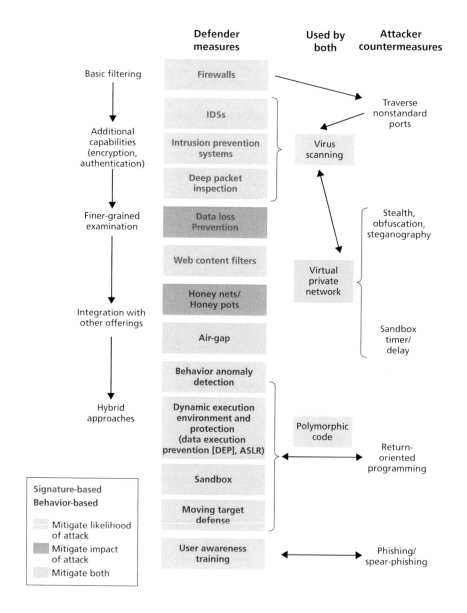

The hope of effectively vulnerability-free software is buttressed by several data points. One is the iOS operating system, which has been much more successful at resisting malware than other mobile device operating systems, such as Android[36]—despite a user base that reflects almost a billion such devices having been sold as of July 2014. Granted, iOS devices lack necessary features (robust multitasking, easy customization) for widespread corporate use,[37] but they at least provide proof that malware-resistant devices are possible. Successive versions of Microsoft operating systems, which constitute most corporate and government foundations, are considered improvements over their predecessors. "Scans of real-world installations show that [Windows] XP systems get infected six times more often than computers running later editions, including Windows 8" (NV, 2014). A high-quality piece of code that goes through a rigorous software development life cycle, such as Microsoft's Security Development Lifecycle,[38] might have fewer easy-to-find vulnerabilities (e.g., bugs found through fuzzing), even if it still contains vulnerabilities that can be found through reverse-engineering or manual inspection. A decrease in active vulnerabilities can also result from faster patch release from vendors, and better defenses, such as the Enhanced Mitigation Experience Toolkit (EMET).[39] The aforementioned president of Vupen observed, "It's definitely getting harder to exploit browsers, especially on Windows 8.1 . . . exploitation is harder and finding zero-days in browsers is harder" (Mimoso, 2014). Indeed, "Left unscathed [at the 2014 Pwn2Own contest] was the highest single prize of the contest, $150,000 for the 'Exploit Unicorn.' This rare beast demanded a specific hack: system-level code execution on a Windows 8.1 x64, in IE 11 x64, with an Enhanced Mitigation Experience Toolkit (EMET) bypass" (Rosenblatt, 2014).

---

[36] This applies to devices that users have decided not to "jail-break."

[37] But see Cunningham (2014).

[38] See Microsoft (2014c).

[39] EMET is a free Microsoft tool to help users deploy and configure a variety of security mitigation technologies (including ASLR and DEP).

Figure 4.2
Both Offense and Defense Scramble to Be First to Find Flaws

Regardless, because of the emphasis of functionality over security, once a technology or device is released to the public, offense and defense sectors start searching for vulnerabilities—starting a measure-countermeasure game of offense (exploit) versus defense (secure). Sometimes the vulnerabilities are exploited first; sometimes defense catches the vulnerability first. Figure 4.2 gives an overview of the cycle of vulnerability discovery.

A Wave of (Connected) Gadgets

Many expect a growing number of devices and objects to be connected in ways that they have not been (and were perhaps never meant to be): for example, the IoT.[40] By the year 2020, the number of connected devices might outnumber the number of connected people by a ratio of 6:1 (Evans, 2011), and 26 billion devices are projected to be connected

---

[40] The title of this section provided with apologies to T. S. Ashton (1961).

considerably in training (as major aerospace companies and defense contractors, in fact, do).

Tools

The use of tools reflects size (larger companies benefit from scale economies), value at risk, and diligence (the ability to use tools effectively). Over time, tools tend to become more attractive on average because more value is at risk and more tools are available, but half of all the tools used in any one year are subject to countermeasures as hackers adapt if and when such tools become popular. In the model, this adaptation causes tools to lose effectiveness over subsequent years. The charts that follow calculate the total number of tools an organization acquires; it includes those subject and not subject to countermeasures.

Figure 5.3 indicates the average number of tools used as a function of the size of the organization (in years 0 and 10). Figure 5.4 indicates the average number of tools used as a function of value at risk (also in years 0 and 10). Figure 5.5 indicates the average number of tools used as a function of diligence (also in years 0 and 10). Part of the reason diligence appears to be a weak factor is that high-diligence organizations get so much value from the first few tools they purchase that

Figure 5.3
Tool Use Rises Sharply as Size Increases

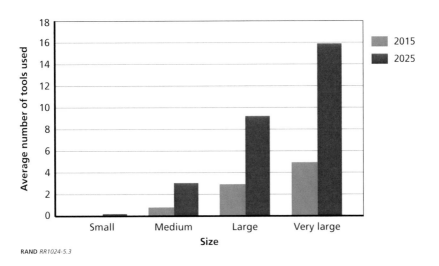

Figure 5.4
Tool Use Also Rises as the Value at Risk Rises

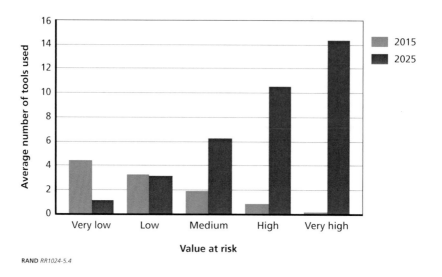

Figure 5.5
Tool Use Is Relatively Insensitive to Diligence

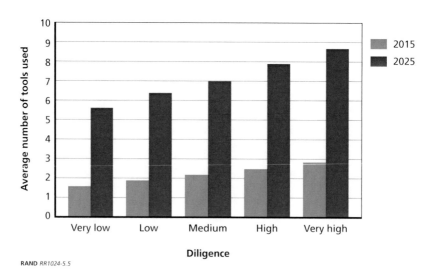

but at the risk of losing the benefits from networking.[13] The number of parts (out of 20) of an organization that are worth air-gapping in year 0

- goes up with size (2.5 parts for very large organizations, 1.5 for large ones, 1 for medium-sized, and 0.5 for small ones)
- goes up with value (3 parts for extra high–value organizations, 2 parts for high-value organizations, 1 part, on average, for the next two, and rarely for the extra low–value organizations)
- has no relationship with diligence (1.5 for all classes).

Year 10 results are very similar—perhaps because the increasingly vigorous use of tools moderates the potential losses arising from cyberattacks and hence the relative value of networking.

The Impact on Annual Costs

Figure 5.6 details the annual losses from cyberattacks and the costs associated with using various instruments of protection: training costs, tool costs, the indirect costs (e.g., loss of network access) associated with restricting BYOD/smart devices, and the indirect costs associated with air-gapping parts of an organization. These four cost categories sum to the total cost of efforts to achieve cybersecurity for an individual organization or for all organizations taken together. The topmost value shown (indicated by large dots) is the amount that losses would have been if no cybersecurity instruments had been used. The presentation of the results posits 2015 as year 0. Except where otherwise indicated, figures in this chapter are normalized so that the losses to cyberattack in 2015 (year 0 in the model) are equal to 1. This helps focus on the percentage change in costs over time and the comparison between various cost categories (e.g., the costs of using instruments relative to the losses from cyberattack).

The most important outcome is that the cost of cyberattacks (overall column height) continues to rise (given the model's param-

---

[13] Because the percentage of an organization's value at risk from cyberattacks from the most sensitive segment was generated randomly for every organization type, the correlation between an organization's attributes and its air-gapping policies is not as clear as if that percentage were the same for all organizations regardless of attributes.

Figure 5.6
Base-Case Losses and Instrument Costs for the Model

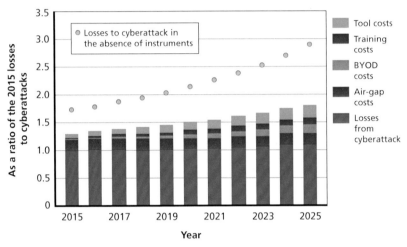

eters) over the next ten years by 38 percent.[14] Most of the increase is accounted for not by the increase in the losses from cyberattacks but from the cost of increasing the efforts to restrain the losses from cyber-attacks: e.g., tools, training, restricting BYOD/smart devices, and air-gapping combined. The total column height (including the yellow/gold losses-in-the-absence-of-instruments portion) in Figure 5.6, however, is a reminder that such instruments kept losses from being worse and rising faster.

The growth rates of expenditures in each of these four lines vary by characteristic, particularly by the size of the organization. Table 5.1 shows results for 2015 (year 0) and 2025 (year 10). The smaller companies suffer fewer losses and see no great need to invest in training, tools, or controlling devices, but retain some requirement for selective air-gapping. The larger companies invest heavily in all four categories, especially tools.

---

[14] As a baseline, the average loss per incident in the model is presumed to rise 5 percent annually, or 63 percent over the ten-year period.

Figure 5.7
Instrument Choices Made by Different Organizations in 2015 and 2025

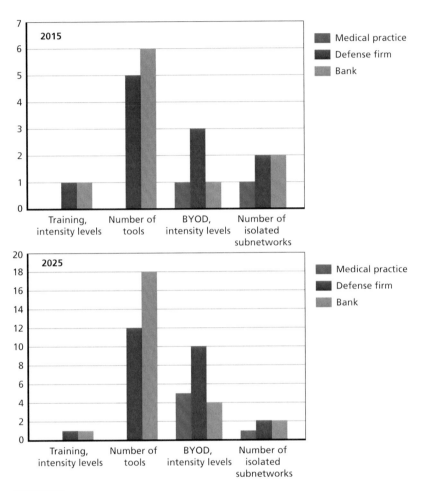

Figure 5.8
Losses Due to Cyberattacks

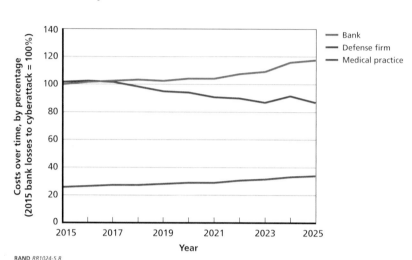

or twice as fast (10 percent) as the 5 percent posited in the base case (even as the cost of using the various instruments remains the same as in the base case)? Not surprisingly, the greater the losses per incident, the higher the incentives to invest in such instruments.

Figure 5.9 shows the ratio of various cost parameters (e.g., losses from cyberattack, tool costs) between the high-growth and the low-growth cases. The orange "Losses from Cyberattack" line represents the growth in the average loss from a successful cyberattack; it is meant just for comparison. The fact that organizations do have access to instruments keeps the overall attack costs from rising as fast as the cost per cyberattack (there are fewer successful cyberattacks). But two categories of instruments rise particularly fast: BYOD/smart device policies (they grow much more severe over time), and the amount of training. Both appear to be quite sensitive to prices.[15]

Underlying External Hardness: We also look at the core equations that define how much loss organizations would suffer from cyberat-

---

[15] Alternatively, the wide distribution in the efficacy of tools and of air-gapping policies (thanks to the introduction of random factors in their value) makes them less sensitive to price.

Figure 5.9
Training Is Very Sensitive to Differences in the Growth Rate of the Loss per Cyberattack

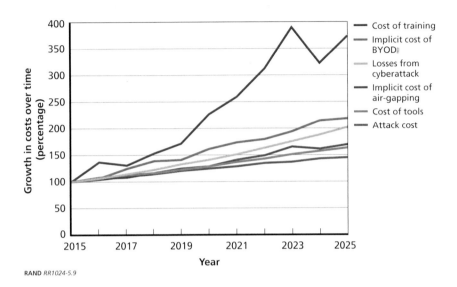

RAND *RR1024-5.9*

tacks. The seven (user-set) parameters are the annual growth rate of computers, the initial (year 0) ratio of devices to computers, the annual growth rate of devices, the vulnerability of computers, the annual change in that vulnerability, the vulnerability of devices, and the annual change in that vulnerability. Because these variables are exogenous, we look at the annual loss from cyberattacks—before and after all the instruments (training, tools, BYOD/smart device restrictions, and air-gapping) come into play.

Figure 5.10 indicates what happens if every computer and device that could be infected were infected. Given the structure of the model, organizations would have only two instruments with which to play: tools and air-gapping (because training and BYOD/smart device restrictions would not raise external hardness up from 0 as long as the organization had at least one computer or device exposed to the outside world).

In Figure 5.11, we play with the ratio of devices to computers: using 0.25 (devices per computers) to represent "fewer," and 1.0 (devices

Figure 5.10
**Both Software Hardness and the Availability of Instruments Are Important
to Managing Losses from Cyberattack**

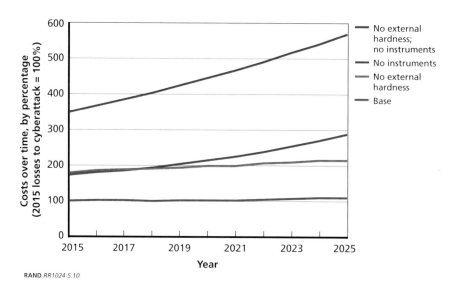

Figure 5.11
**The More Smart Devices (Relative to Computers), the Greater the Losses
from Cyberattack**

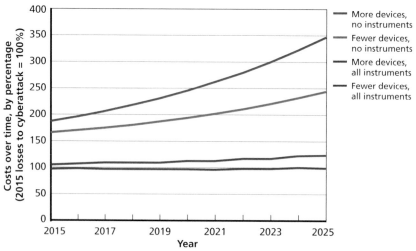

per computers) to represent "more." Shifting the ratio has a significant effect on pre-instrument and post-instrument attack costs (recall, the instruments are tools and air-gapping).

Growth Rate of Computers: We also varied the growth rate in the number of computers in the model, using four alternative rates (Figure 5.12): 2.5 percent (very slow), 5 percent (measured), 10 percent (baseline), and 20 percent (fast). With varied growth rates come varied cost curves. Unlike the case when changing the device/computer ratio, the ability of instruments to moderate the large difference is substantially less (if computer use grows very slowly, pre-instrument losses from cyberattack decline by one-quarter relative to the base case, but post-instrument overall costs drop by one-half).

Growth Rate of Devices: Differences in the annual growth rates of devices—15 percent and 40 percent were modeled (compared with 25 percent in the base case)—are also important (even if the effect is exaggerated because the base-case growth rate for devices, and thus the variations off the base case, are wider than they are for computer

Figure 5.12
Alternative Growth Rates in the Number of Computers Have a Large Impact on Losses from Cyberattack That Persists Even After Instruments Are Used

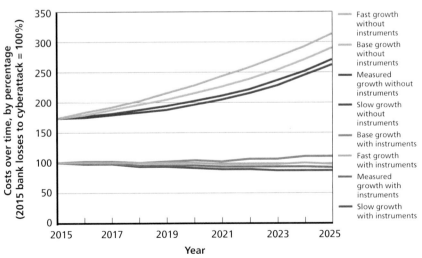

growth). Although the pre-instrument costs vary greatly (a faster growth rate represents a near doubling of costs), the post-instrument cost differences are smaller. The reason is that one of the instruments is to suppress the proliferation of devices (in the model, the population of computers is exogenous). See Figure 5.13.

Substitution of Computers by Devices and Vice Versa: In Figure 5.14, we changed the growth rate of computers and devices together. Instead of the number of computers growing by 10 percent per year and the number of devices growing by 25 percent per year, we examined a range of growth rates. In one run, 5 percent was subtracted from the growth rate of computers and added to the growth rate of smart devices; in the other run, the opposite shift was made. As a general rule, substitution from computers to devices yields a lower set of losses to cyber-attack; this result is achieved, however, because a world of more-available devices is also a world in which organizations optimize to restrict device use more and thus suffer more costs from limiting the usefulness of their networks (the model's parameters reflect the fact that devices are harder to hack into than computers are). The net costs—

Figure 5.13
Alternative Growth Rates in the Number of Devices Have a Large Impact on Losses from Cyberattack, but Instruments Can Sharply Reduce the Difference

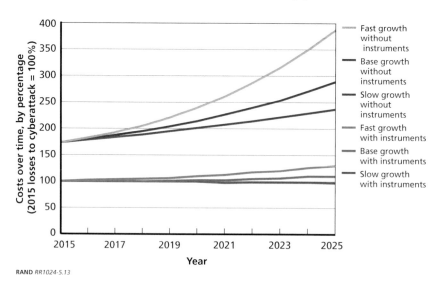

Figure 5.14
Shifting Growth from Computers to Devices Reduces the Losses from Cyberattacks but Only After BYOD/Smart Device Policies Are Taken into Account

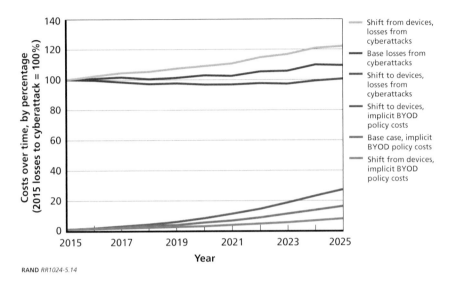

RAND RR1024-5.14

losses plus the cost of implementing security measures—are roughly the same regardless of whether substitution takes place.

Baseline Vulnerability of Computers (but Not Devices): We then examined differences that result in playing with the vulnerability of computers in year 0: "Loose" represented a computer whose odds of being penetrated was twice that of the base case, and "tight" represented one whose odds were half that. This, too, made a huge difference. Indeed, this is one of the few parameters that narrows rather than widens over time. Of greater note was that the cost difference, after instruments were applied, was at least or even larger than the cost difference before instruments were applied. This is illustrated in Figure 5.15.

Growth Rate of Software Improvement in Computers: A similar tale, in Figure 5.16, might be told by varying the rate at which software improves. In the base case, the odds that a single computer can be penetrated are reduced by 15 percent per year; in the test cases, the improvement rate is either twice as fast or twice as slow. Such differ-

Figure 5.15
Baseline Software Vulnerability Makes a Big Difference in Losses from Cyberattack That Instruments Cannot Counteract

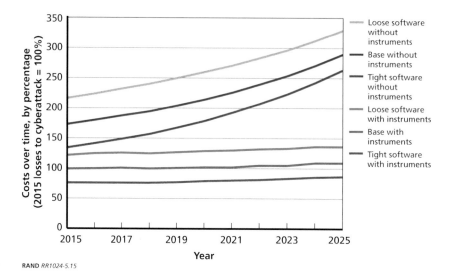

RAND RR1024-5.15

Figure 5.16
Changes in the Improvement Rate of Software Vulnerability Make a Big Difference in Losses from Cyberattack That Instruments Cannot Counteract

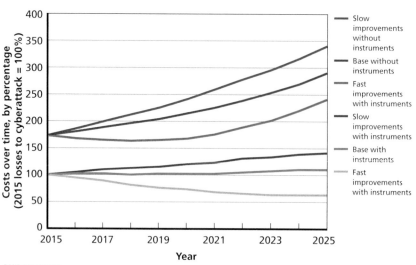

RAND RR1024-5.16

ences initially have a large effect on the (pre-instrument) external hardness of organizations, but, in the longer run, the curves are dominated by the likelihood of penetrating an organization through its noncomputer devices. However, the differences persist when looking at post-instrument external hardness, in large part because one of the instruments, again, is restricting the proliferation of noncomputer devices. Thus, by year 10, the difference between twice as fast and twice as slow is well over 3:1 in terms of the cost of cyberattack. The upper lines represent pre-instrument losses; the lower lines, post-instrument losses.

Baseline Vulnerability of Devices: If the variable to be tinkered with is the vulnerability of devices, the converse story can be told. Figure 5.17 examines a base case, an alternative in which devices were twice as resistant to attack, and an alternative in which devices were half as resistant to attack. The difference expands as the years progress. However, when instruments are factored in, the difference is substantially reduced, again, in large part because one of the policy instruments is the ability to reduce the device count.

Figure 5.17
Baseline Device Vulnerability Makes a Difference to Losses from Cyberattack That Instruments *Can* Counteract

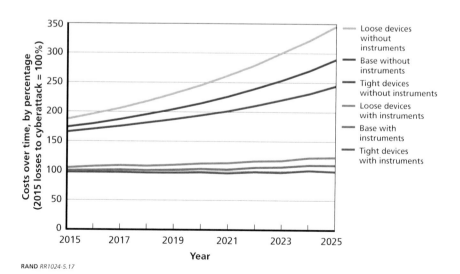

Growth Rate of Software Improvement in Devices: Finally, a similar story emerges if the rate of improvement in device software is charted. Over a ten-year period, software quality makes a great deal of difference before instruments are taken into account—and a significant, albeit attenuated difference, after the instruments are applied. See Figure 5.18.

Training

Training Costs: Figure 5.19 moots training costs that are, alternatively, twice and then half as expensive as in the base case. The more expensive cybersecurity training is, the less that will be purchased, and the greater the losses that can be expected from a cyberattack. Training costs are quite sensitive to the price of training (far more money would be spent on training if the costs were lower, and vice versa). Such training would have a significant effect on the penetrability of computers and hence the external hardness of an organization. Unfortunately, most of the benefit from fewer cyberattacks would be eaten up by the additional cost of training, leaving organizations only somewhat better

Figure 5.18
**Changes in the Improvement Rate of Device Vulnerability Make a Big
Difference in Losses from Cyberattack That Instruments *Can* Counteract**

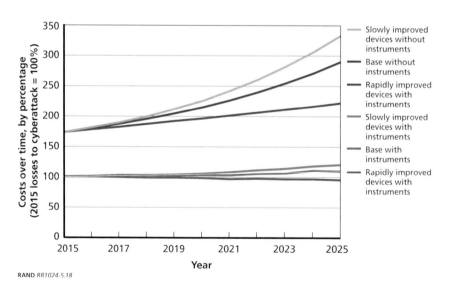

Figure 5.19
Changing the Price of Training Reduces the Losses from Cyberattack but Increases Costs

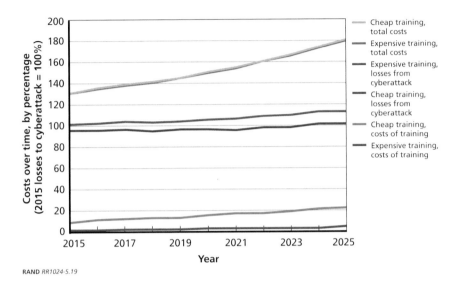

off if the cost of training fell (or only somewhat worse off if the cost of training rose).

Cost of an Increase in Level of Training: In Figure 5.20, we look at the impact of doubling or halving the efficacy of the training tools (measured by how much each level of training reduced the effective number of exposed computers). Improving the efficacy of training has a substantial impact on the losses suffered as a result of cyberattacks. Unfortunately, when factoring in the additional cost of training to take advantage of its increased efficacy (or reduced cost of training if efficacy were lower), most of the difference, again, disappeared. Some of this is an artifact of the model's design, in which training decisions precede decisions to isolate subnetworks. The difference associated with doubling the efficacy of training is far larger than the difference associated with halving the efficacy of training.

Figure 5.20
Changing the Efficacy of Training Reduces Losses from Cyberattack but Increases Costs

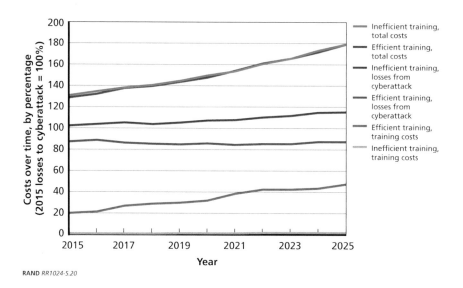

Tools

The Number of Tools Offered per Year: In the base model, two new tools are introduced every year. What happens if four tools are introduced every year? The most direct effect is that an organization would have a larger choice, allowing it to substitute more-effective tools for some of those whose effectiveness was just middling. Overall costs from insecurity in cyberspace would decline. By year 10, the cost of cyberattacks themselves would decline substantially, although half of the savings are eaten up by the cost of buying and operating the new tools required to suppress the growth of cybersecurity costs (offset, in turn, by slight reductions in the cost of imposing restrictions on BYOD/smart device use and connectivity). See Figure 5.21.

The Effectiveness of Tools: In the base model, the underlying effectiveness of a tool is 2.5 percent, meaning that the use of each tool (including those for which countermeasures are effective and those for which countermeasures are not effective and adjusted for its tool rating and for the diligence of the organization) reduces the cost of cyber-

Figure 5.21
Increasing the Number of New Tools Reduces Losses from Cyberattack but Increases Expenditures on Tools Somewhat

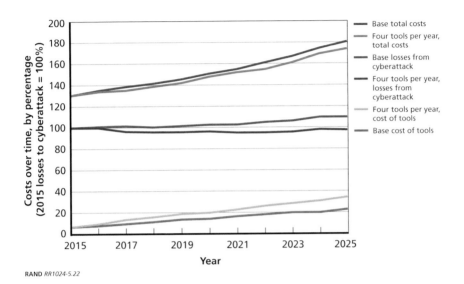

RAND RR1024-5.22

attacks by that much. What happens if the effectiveness of each tool were doubled to 5 percent? This causes a substantial shift in the cost associated with cyberattacks, offset only modestly by an increase in the cost of using more tools, as shown in Figure 5.22. Correspondingly, reducing the effectiveness of tools by half raises the total cost of cyber-space insecurity by raising the losses from attacks significantly, offset somewhat by the fact that fewer tools are purchased.

The Price of Tools: Changing the prices of the tools—doubling them (pricey) or halving them (cheap)—does not seem to have nearly as much *direct* impact as Figure 5.23 shows. Indirectly, the impact of an expensive tool is to force organizations to reduce connectivity (thus incurring implicit costs); the reverse is true if tools are cheap. Organizations spend less money on cheap tools, but their expenses do not rise that much if tools are pricey (in part because fewer are purchased).

The Tool Countermeasurable Parameter: Playing with the counter-measure parameter (Figure 5.24), we see that the decline in the effectiveness of those tools subject to countermeasures makes little differ-

Figure 5.22
The Effectiveness of Tools Has Significant Effects on the Costs and Losses Associated with Cyberattack

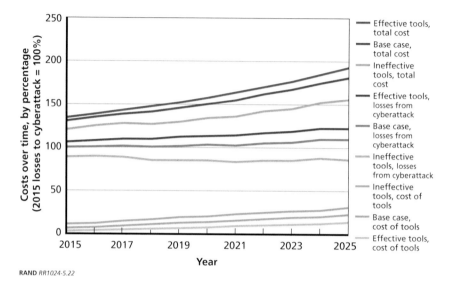

Figure 5.23
Tool Prices Also Have Significant Effects on the Costs and Losses Associated with Cyberattack

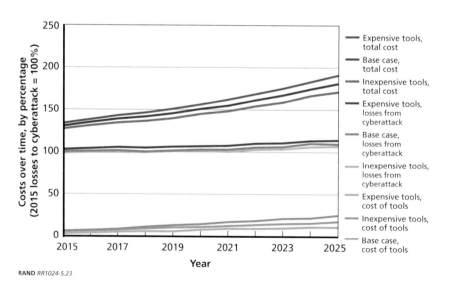

Figure 5.24
Even Weak Countermeasures to Tools Affect Losses from Cyberattack

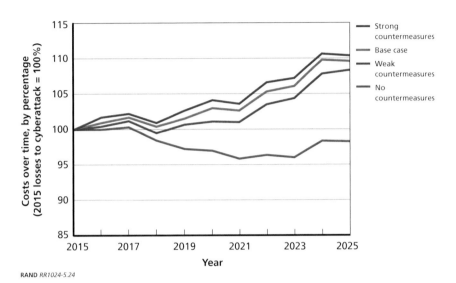

ence. The base case is 75 percent; examining test cases of 50 percent (weak countermeasure effects) and 100 percent (strong countermeasure effects) indicates very little effect on the losses from cyberattack—a difference of no more than 2 percent by the tenth year (even if larger during some intermediate years). This might be because, at even weak rates of countermeasures, nine of the top ten tools available to defenders will be those tools from past years whose value has not decreased as a result of countermeasures.

BYOD/Smart Device Policies and Air-Gapping

Variations in the value of connectivity (from twice to half that of the base case)—hence the cost of wielding such instruments as restrictive BYOD/smart device policies and air-gapping—have a tangible but modest effect on the costs of cybersecurity. It works in the expected direction: The more value from connectivity, the fewer connectivity-blocking instruments merit employment and thus the greater the losses from cyberattacks. The actual cost of restrictions, however, is the same, suggesting that both instruments have a cost elasticity of

Figure 5.25
The Less Networking Is Necessary, the Lower the Losses from Cyberattack

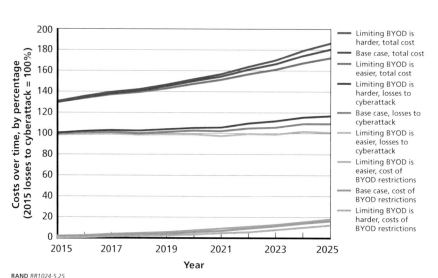

roughly 1 (the number of burdens imposed falls as the cost per burden rises). Figure 5.25 portrays the losses from cyberattacks and the costs of restrictions.

The Efficacy of BYOD/Smart Device Policies: Similar, but stronger, effects arise when looking at the efficacy of BYOD/smart device policies—again doubling (efficient) and halving (inefficient) the ability of each level of severity on the implicit population of devices. Over a ten-year period, there is a substantial improvement in the losses associated with cyberattacks that is somewhat offset by the increased costs of implementing BYOD/smart device policies. Figure 5.26 shows the total cost of cyberinsecurity (the cost of attacks plus the cost of preventions), the losses from cyberattack (alone), and the cost of BYOD/smart device policies.

Air-Gapping: Costs appear to be relatively sensitive to changes in the various parameters associated with air-gapping. Changing (that is, doubling or halving) the factor that converts the degree of air-gapping into a monetary cost (in terms of the lost value from connectivity) has a substantial effect on the losses to cyberattack and retains most

Figure 5.26
How Changing the Efficacy of BYOD Policies Affects the Losses from Cyberattacks with Only Modest Offsetting Costs

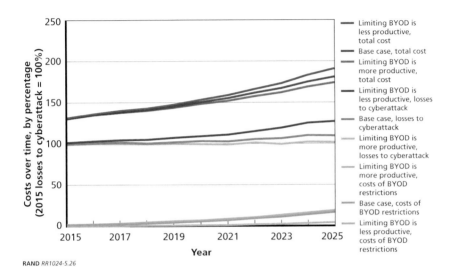

RAND RR1024-5.26

Figure 5.27
Total Costs Go Down When Air-Gapping Becomes Cheaper

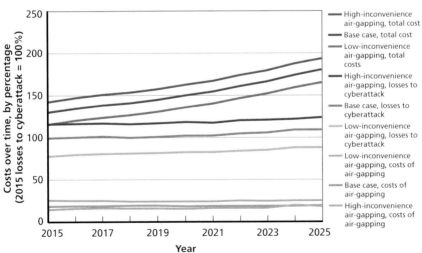

RAND RR1024-5.27

of that even after changes in the cost of using instruments has been factored in (see Figure 5.27).

Conclusions

Although the model yields a plethora of results, the following appear worthy of note.

The various instruments that organizations can use to control the losses from cyberattack are collectively powerful. Yet much of what they do is transfer costs from cyberattack losses to the cost of the effort necessary to manage losses; for all model years, roughly 40 percent of the reduced losses are offset by increased costs associated with using such instruments (direct acquisition and usage costs plus implicit reduction in the value of networking). Developing instruments that offer better cost-effectiveness ratios would be useful.

The size of the organization matters greatly to its optimal strategy. Small organizations benefit from circumstances and policies that reduce their attack surfaces (e.g., BYOD/smart device restrictions). Larger organizations need a panoply of instruments to keep costs under control.

Although instruments are important, exogenous factors—notably the quality of software used by organizations—have a very large effect on the losses from cyberattack (and at relatively low cost compared with the cost of cybersecurity tools). There need to be better mechanisms to convey the interests organizations have in the quality of code to those responsible for writing such code.

Over time, the potential influence of smart devices on cybersecurity will approach and perhaps exceed the influence of computers on cybersecurity. The introduction of networked computers into organizations in the 1980s and 1990s was allowed to happen without a very sophisticated understanding of the security implications. It would be useful if the same mistake were not made with smart devices.

The model posits that security implications arising from the growth of the number of smart devices can be managed by policies that limit the connections between smart devices and networks. This is why